THE
VICTORIOUS
CHRISTIAN

Inheriting the Promises

Jon von Ernst

New Harbor Press

RAPID CITY, SD

Ernst/New Harbor Press
1601 Mt. Rushmore Rd, Ste 3288
Rapid City, SD 57701
www.NewHarborPress.com

The Victorious Christian/Jon von Ernst. -- 1st ed.
ISBN 978-1-63357-349-9

Correspondence may be addressed to the author at: thepureword@yahoo.com

CONTENTS

PREFACE

All glory and honor for any benefit that may result from anyone reading this book goes directly to God the Father and His Son, Jesus Christ our Lord!

I would, however, like to acknowledge the many tools that He used, not only to prompt me to begin this writing, but also to encourage me to complete it. He provided much encouragement and stimulation of thought through the fellowship of many dear brothers and sisters in the Lord. He also provided invaluable assistance from my wife Linda.

It is my prayer that this book would help unbelievers to come to saving faith in Jesus Christ our Lord. I pray, also, that Christians would find encouragement in this book to look to Jesus for everything they need to live lives that are holy and pleasing unto the Lord, that they might continue steadfast to the end and have confidence at Christ's appearing.

You will notice that each chapter of this book is followed by a list of discussion questions. These are designed to enrich the reader's understanding of the truths presented in each chapter. These questions are also intended to be used as a resource to stimulate thought and discussion among the members of Bible study and fellowship groups that utilize this book as an aide in their spiritual growth.

The first section of this book is intended to help believers come to a basic understanding of some fundamental truths for the Christian life. This section of the book is also to encourage believers as they grow in their faith and in their knowledge of our Lord Jesus Christ.

The second section of this book is to turn the focus of the believers to the vision of the church as the bride of Christ. It is intended to give them a glimpse of God's eternal purpose for the church and their place in it as a member of the body of Christ.

The purpose of the third section of this book is to focus on the importance of remaining faithful unto the end. It is intended to encourage every believer to keep their eyes fixed on Jesus, no matter how unsettling the things taking place in the world may appear to be. We are to encourage each other, reminding one another that God is in control, that Jesus has won the victory and that all who walk in faithful obedience to Him will emerge victorious.

May all who read this book find in it a new realization of the pressing need to be prepared for the soon return of our glorious Lord and Savior, Jesus Christ!

—Jon von Ernst

INTRODUCTION

It is important that the reader understand the danger of accepting the teachings of this author, or any other author, pastor, or teacher at face value. No person's teachings should be blindly accepted. When we, without question, accept anyone's teachings, we place ourselves in danger of being led astray. There are many false teachers in the world and in the church today. It is essential that we try the spirits and that we take any teaching, no matter how famous or highly revered the teacher may be, to the Scriptures for verification. This author encourages you to take the teachings of this book to the Scriptures and search them out diligently.

When we take teachings to the Scriptures, it is important to look up and review the context of the passages that the teacher has referred to. It may be even more important to allow the Spirit to direct us to passages that appear to contradict the conclusions presented by the teacher. Usually there is more than one perspective presented in Scripture for any individual truth. This is due to the incredible depth of the manifold wisdom of God. It is the tendency of natural man to see, at most, only one side of any truth presented in Scripture. It is therefore necessary for the reader, the listener, to look to the Holy Spirit to reveal more than just one aspect of any truth in question. We should desire God to reveal to us as many aspects of the specific truth as He is willing to show us, and that we are able and prepared to receive.

Our initial desire in searching out in the Scriptures the truths that are being taught is to verify if the teachings do in fact have a scriptural basis and are properly applied. Our secondary goal is to broaden our understanding of the specific truth being taught by seeing that truth from other perspectives, thereby deepening our understanding of our God and of His ways. As we come to see various aspects of any truth, we will become more accepting of other believers, and of their individual understanding of the truths that they have come to believe and embrace. This will enable us to more effectively maintain the unity of the Spirit and reduce the tendency to separate ourselves from other believers simply because we have stumbled upon some teaching about which there are different understandings.

It is important for all of us to realize that none of us has all understanding or all knowledge of the truths presented in Scripture. At best, we see in part, and we understand in part. We are all disciples. We are all students. We are all in the process of learning. The only way any of us can learn is if we begin by humbling ourselves and admit that we do not have all the answers. We need to consider others as better than ourselves and realize that if we have an ear to hear, God can teach us by His Spirit through the speaking of any brother or sister. When we think too highly of ourselves, we have greatly reduced our ability to learn.

Our ultimate goal, in coming to the Scriptures, is to be fed. We must come to the Scriptures as those that are hungry for the living word of God, Jesus Christ our Lord. Our desire should be to know Him. May God give us the grace and the hunger to hear God's speaking by His Spirit through the Scriptures and through every brother or sister that we fellowship with. Perhaps if we are hungry enough, God will feed us with more of Christ, that at His return, we may know Him and be found in Him!

May we be those that are truly taught by the Holy Spirit and not by men.

—Jon von Ernst

SECTION I – BASIC TRUTHS FOR SPIRITUAL GROWTH

UNDERSTANDING SCRIPTURE

Some people spend much of their lives trying to understand the Bible, the Scriptures. Others, seeing little value in the Scriptures, have spent little or no time reading them, much less trying to understand them. So, how important is it to understand Scripture? What difference does it make whether I understand the Scriptures or not?

In Matthew 13:18-23, Jesus spoke to His disciples saying, "Hear then the parable of the sower. When anyone hears the word of the kingdom and does not understand it, the evil one comes and snatches away what has been sown in his heart. This is the one on whom seed was sown beside the road. The one on whom seed was sown on the rocky places, this is the man who hears the word and immediately receives it with joy; yet he has no firm root in himself, but is only temporary, and when affliction or persecution arises because of the word, immediately he falls away. And the one on whom seed was sown among the thorns, this is the man who hears the word, and the worry of the world and the deceitfulness of wealth choke the word, and it becomes unfruitful. And the one on whom seed was sown on the good soil, this is the man who hears the word and understands it, who indeed bears fruit and brings forth, some a hundredfold, some sixty, and some thirty."

In this passage, Jesus makes it very clear that understanding plays a vital role in both salvation and in being fruitful and growing unto maturity. Notice the evil one snatches away the seed that has been sown in the heart of the one that does not understand. However, the good soil is the heart of the man who not only hears the word, but also understands it. The man who hears and understands bears fruit and brings forth fruit in abundance.

Paul writes in Romans 9:13, "Just as it is written, 'JACOB I LOVED, BUT ESAU I HATED.'" Jacob and Esau were brothers. Esau was the oldest and therefore had the birthright of inheritance.

Many people have wondered why God would have displayed such apparent favoritism, loving one and hating the other. Genesis 25:29-34 gives us some insight as to why God had this attitude toward Jacob and Esau. It says, "Once when Jacob was cooking some stew, Esau came in from the open country, famished. He said to Jacob, 'Quick, let me have some of that red stew! I'm famished!' ... Jacob replied, 'First sell me your birthright.' 'Look, I am about to die,' Esau said. 'What good is the birthright to me?' But Jacob said, 'Swear to me first.' So he swore an oath to him, selling his birthright to Jacob. Then Jacob gave Esau some bread and some lentil stew. He ate and drank, and then got up and left. So Esau despised his birthright" (NIV).

God favored Jacob because Jacob understood the birthright. Because Jacob understood the birthright, he realized its significance. This enabled Jacob to value the birthright. Esau, however, did not understand the birthright or its value and sold it for a bowl of stew and some bread. Lacking understanding, Esau despised his birthright. Because of his lack of understanding, Esau was deceived into despising and selling his birthright.

In Matthew 22:29, Jesus told the religious leaders that they were deceived. "Jesus answered and said to them, 'You are mistaken, not understanding the Scriptures nor the power of God.'" There are some people today who know the Scriptures very well, including religious leaders, yet they also may be deceived.

In John 5:38-40, Jesus again confronted the religious leaders and revealed how badly deceived they were. He said to them, "You don't have His word living in you, because you don't believe the One He sent. You pore over the Scriptures because you think you have eternal life in them, yet they testify about Me. And you are not willing to come to Me that you may have life" (HCSB).

I remember seeing a quotation engraved on the archway over the entrance to a chapel at a Bible college. It was taken from 2 Timothy 2:15. It said, "Study to show thyself approved unto God." The implication of course is that the harder you study, the more God will approve of you. However, the word translated "study" in this passage does not really mean to study. It literally means to be diligent, to be eager, to act promptly, as in when God speaks, be quick to obey.

The context here is that Paul is encouraging Timothy that he must be diligent to accurately teach the word of truth. The verse actually says, "Be diligent to present yourself approved to God as a workman who does not need to be ashamed, accurately handling the word of truth."

Paul gave this warning because some had deviated from the truth and had become false teachers. It is good, whenever you hear someone share something, to search the Scriptures to verify whether their teaching is correct or not. If their teaching is not accurate, they should be corrected.

Paul continues in verse 21, referring to the false teachings, "Therefore, if anyone cleanses himself from these things, he will be a vessel for honor, sanctified, useful to the Master, prepared for every good work." Paul continues in verses 24 and 25, "The Lord's bond-servant must not be quarrelsome, but be kind to all, able to teach, patient when wronged, with gentleness correcting those who are in opposition, if perhaps God may grant them repentance leading to the knowledge of the truth."

Paul is telling Timothy not to get caught up in foolish disputes that cause arguments and divisions. He wants him to correctly handle the word of truth and stay focused on the basics of obedience, living a holy life, loving the brothers and maintaining the unity of the Spirit. We must understand that we cannot argue anyone into believing the truth. It is the Holy Spirit that reveals truth.

In 2 Timothy 3:1-5, Paul warns that in the last days people will be "lovers of pleasure rather than lovers of God, holding to a form of godliness, although they have denied its power; Avoid such men as these." Because they will not come to Jesus and trust Him completely, they do not know the power of God and cannot really know the Scriptures. Therefore, they are deceived, holding to a form of religion, but denying its power.

I Corinthians 2:6-14 says, "Yet we do speak wisdom among those who are mature; a wisdom, however, not of this age nor of the rulers of this age, who are passing away; but we speak God's wisdom in a mystery, the hidden wisdom which God predestined before the ages to our glory; the wisdom which none of the rulers of this age has understood; for if they had understood it they would not have crucified the Lord of glory; but just as it is written, 'THINGS WHICH EYE HAS NOT SEEN AND EAR HAS NOT HEARD, AND which HAVE NOT ENTERED THE HEART OF MAN, ALL THAT GOD HAS PREPARED FOR THOSE WHO LOVE HIM.'

"For to us God revealed them through the Spirit; for the Spirit searches all things, even the depths of God. For who among men knows the thoughts of a man except the spirit of the man which is in him? Even so the thoughts of God no one knows except the Spirit of God.

"Now we have received, not the spirit of the world, but the Spirit who is from God, so that we may know the things freely given to us by God, which things we also speak, not in words taught by human wisdom, but in those taught by the Spirit, combining spiritual thoughts with spiritual words. But a natural man does not accept the things of the Spirit of God, for they are foolishness to him; and he cannot understand them, because they are spiritually appraised."

The term "it is written" is used to refer to something in the Scriptures, especially the Old Testament. The Scriptures, both the Old and the New Testaments, were written by men as they were directed by the Holy Spirit (2 Peter 1:21). Therefore, the Scriptures are spiritual and must be spiritually understood.

The natural man is not able, not having the Spirit of Christ within him, to understand the Scriptures, because, being spiritual, they are discerned only through the Spirit. They just don't make sense to the natural man. It does not matter how well educated you are or how many degrees you may have. Without the Spirit, you do not have the ability to understand the Scriptures.

Many people today, however, are sold on the importance of studying the Scriptures, of poring over them, of analyzing them, because they think that in doing so they will find a deeper understanding of God and of His ways. But they are unwilling to come to and completely trust in the One of whom the Scriptures speak, the One that has the power to give them life and to give them understanding.

If we know the power of God, Jesus Christ as the Holy Spirit dwelling in our human spirit, God, by this power, will teach us all that is ours in Christ. He will reveal the truth in Scripture to us.

In 2 Corinthians 3:6, Paul says God "made us adequate as servants of a new covenant, not of the letter but of the Spirit; for the letter kills, but the Spirit gives life." When we come to the Scriptures, we should not come to study them, trying according to our own natural understanding to learn what they mean. If we do, we will indeed find that the letter kills. Solomon, in his great wisdom, warns in Proverbs 3:5, "Trust in the LORD with all your heart, and do not lean on your own understanding." Then in Ecclesiastes 12:12, he exposes that the result of "much study is a weariness of the flesh" (WEB).

Instead of studying and analyzing, we should come to the Scriptures to be fed. In John 6:35 Jesus said, "I am the bread of life; he who comes to Me will not hunger, and he who believes in Me will never thirst."

In John 6:47-51, Jesus said, "Truly, truly, I say to you, he who believes has eternal life. I am the bread of life. Your fathers ate the manna in the wilderness, and they died. This is the bread which comes down out of heaven, so that one may eat of it and not die. I am the living bread that came down out of heaven; if anyone eats of this bread, he will live forever."

Jesus says in John 6:63, "It is the Spirit who gives life; the flesh profits nothing; the words that I have spoken to you are spirit and are life." When we come to the Scriptures, we must not come to understand by means of our natural intellect. If we do, we will experience death. We must come to the Scriptures, in spirit, to hear Christ speak to us, that we might receive more of His life and be filled with His Spirit.

When we come to the Scriptures, we must come with the desire and the expectation that God would breathe on the Scriptures and make them come alive to us. 2 Timothy 3:16-17 says, "Every Scripture, when inspired [breathed upon] by God is profitable for teaching, for reproof, for correction, and for instruction concerning righteousness so that the man of God may be completely prepared for accomplishing every good work" (TFLV).

We need to come to the Scriptures and allow them, through God's breathing on them, and through the Spirit's speaking, to lead us into a deeper knowledge of our Lord Jesus Christ. As we are feeding on the living Word and filled with His Spirit, we will find ourselves saying along with Jeremiah, "Your words were found, and I ate them. Your words were to me a joy and the rejoicing of my heart" (Jeremiah 15:16, WEB).

When our children were small and still at home, my wife would always tell them, "Eat slower, chew your food well." This is how we should come to the Scriptures. We should come to them as those that are hungry, hungry for the "living bread of life."

We should feed on them slowly, enjoying every bite, getting as much out of them as possible. We should ruminate on them, as a sheep chewing its cud. We should meditate on them, patiently waiting for God to breathe on them, and for His Spirit to break them open and make them a blessing to us.

We will discover that the Word of God is not dead letter. It is not just a written document. The Word of God is the living, breathing person of Jesus Christ. He is indwelling the heart of every true believer. He is also that germ of life embedded in every grain of Scripture. We must allow the Lord, as the Spirit, to break open that grain of Scripture and release the living Word embedded within it. When the Lord does this, we are richly fed.

In John 14:15-17, Jesus tells His disciples, "If you love Me, you will keep My commandments. I will ask the Father, and He will give you another Helper, that He may be with you forever; that is the Spirit of Truth, whom the world cannot receive, because it does not see Him or know Him, but you know Him because He abides with you and will be in you."

In John 14:25, Jesus told His disciples, "These things I have spoken to you while abiding with you. But the Helper, the Holy Spirit, whom the Father will send in My name, He will teach you all things, and bring to your remembrance all that I said to you."

In Acts 19:1-4, Paul comes to Ephesus and meets some disciples, about 12 in number. He asks them, "Did you receive the Holy Spirit when you believed?" And they said to him, "No, we have not even heard whether there is a Holy Spirit." And he said, "Into what then were you baptized?" And they said, "Into John's baptism." Paul said, "John baptized with the baptism of repentance, telling the people to believe in Him who was coming after him, that is, in Jesus."

I have met many people who claim to be Christians who know nothing of the Holy Spirit. Romans 8:9 says, "If anyone does not have the Spirit of Christ, he does not belong to Him." In John 3:5-6 Jesus says, "Truly, truly, I say to you, unless one is born of water and the Spirit he cannot enter into the kingdom of God. That which is born of the flesh is flesh, and that which is born of the Spirit is spirit."

When you are born again, your spirit is made alive when the Holy Spirit, the Spirit of Christ, comes to dwell in you, and you become a new creation. Your life and your desires begin to be totally changed, transformed. You become a new creation that delights to feed on the living bread, the Word of God, Jesus Christ our Lord! Being born again is a life changing, earth shattering experience.

It is impossible to understand the Scriptures or to know the power of God without being born again. We must have the Spirit of Christ. Only then will this indwelling Holy Spirit open the Scriptures and reveal the deep, hidden things of God to us. Truly, the Holy Spirit will teach us all things and empower us to be victorious Christians!

Chapter 1 Discussion Questions: Understanding Scripture

1. What is the difference between the one that understands the word and the one that does not?
2. Why did God love Jacob and hate Esau?
3. Why were the religious leaders deceived?
4. What must we do to be useful to the Master, prepared for every good work?
5. Why must we not quarrel, but be gentle when dealing with opponents or unbelievers?
6. How do we know that the rulers of this age did not understand the hidden wisdom of God?
7. Why has God given His Holy Spirit to believers?
8. Why does the natural man not accept the things of the Spirit?
9. How were the Scriptures written?

10. Why is it necessary to be born again in order to understand Scripture?
11. What is the power of God?
12. Who is the Word of God?
13. Who is the Spirit of truth?
14. Who will give us understanding, teaching us all things?

....

RECEIVING THE HOLY SPIRIT

"While Apollos was in Corinth, Paul traveled through the interior regions and came to Ephesus. He found some disciples and asked them, 'Did you receive the Holy Spirit when you believed?' 'No,' they told him, 'we haven't even heard that there is a Holy Spirit.' 'Then what baptism were you baptized with?' he asked them. 'With John's baptism,' they replied. Paul said, 'John baptized with a baptism of repentance, telling the people that they should believe in the One who would come after him, that is, in Jesus.' When they heard this, they were baptized in the name of the Lord Jesus. And when Paul had laid his hands on them, the Holy Spirit came on them, and they began to speak in other languages and to prophesy. Now there were about 12 men in all" (Acts 19:1-7, HCSB).

There was apparently something in the behavior or the appearance of these disciples that troubled Paul and caused him to ask them whether they had received the Holy Spirit when they believed. Perhaps it was their attitude, or perhaps the things they said. Apparently, there was something that gave Paul the impression that they were not walking according to the Spirit, but according to the flesh. Perhaps they were legalistic and attempting to be justified according to the law.

Paul later writes to the church in Ephesus, "Follow God's example, therefore, as dearly loved children and walk in the way of love, just as Christ loved us and gave himself up for us as a fragrant offering and sacrifice to God. But among you there must not be even a hint of sexual immorality, or of any kind of impurity, or of greed, because these are improper for God's holy people. Nor should there be obscenity, foolish talk or coarse joking, which are out of place, but rather thanksgiving.

"For of this you can be sure: No immoral, impure or greedy person—such a person is an idolater—has any inheritance in the kingdom of Christ and of God. Let no one deceive you with empty words, for because of such things God's wrath comes on those who are disobedient. Therefore do not be partners with them. For you were once darkness, but now you are light in the Lord. Live as children of light" (Ephesians 5:1-8, NIV).

Perhaps Paul wrote this to the church in Ephesus out of concern about what he had earlier observed when he met the 12 disciples of John's baptism of repentance. The gospel of repentance addresses the sins that we have committed with an outward washing by baptism in water and challenges us to turn back to God. However, it does nothing to cleanse our conscience from sin, nor does it free us from the fallen sinful nature of our old man or empower us to live a holy life.

Paul knew that if we are to walk worthy of the Lord and be pleasing unto Him, if we are to live victorious Christian lives, we must have our consciences cleansed and we must be set free from the dominion of sin in our lives. But how can we experience this cleansing and this deliverance from the control that sin has over us?

The only way to enter into this experience is to believe in Jesus and be baptized by Him with the Holy Spirit. It is only by being born again, by having the Spirit of Christ indwell us and abide in us that we could have our consciences cleansed and be set free from the dominion of sin to live holy lives that would glorify God.

Paul says in Romans 8:9, "If anyone has not the Spirit of Christ, he does not belong to Him." It is clear from this verse that what we need, to become a Christian, is the Holy Spirit. Without the Holy Spirit, we will never be able to please God. Without the Spirit, we are not genuine Christians.

Jesus said in John 3:6, "That which is born of the flesh is flesh, and that which is born of the Spirit is spirit." We must be born again. Our spirit must be born or made alive by the Holy Spirit coming to dwell in, abide in, our spirit.

The question then is, how can we receive the Holy Spirit? What do we have to do to receive the Holy Spirit, to be born again? Are there some secret words we must say? Is there a certain prayer we must repeat? Is there some kind of penance we must do to make ourselves acceptable so that the Holy Spirit will be given to us?

Luke 11:9-13 tells us that Jesus said to His disciples, "I tell you, keep asking, and it will be given you. Keep seeking, and you will find. Keep knocking, and it will be opened to you. For everyone who asks receives. He who seeks finds. To him who knocks it will be opened.

"Which of you fathers, if your son asks for bread, will give him a stone? Or if he asks for a fish, he won't give him a snake instead of a fish, will he? Or if he asks for an egg, he won't give him a scorpion, will he? If you then, being evil, know how to give good gifts to your children, how much more will your heavenly Father give the Holy Spirit to those who ask him?" (WEB).

It is clear from this passage that our Father, who is in heaven, wants to give us what is most needful for us to live lives that are totally pleasing to Him. Our heavenly Father wants to give us the Holy Spirit. All He requires is that we, believing in the Lord Jesus Christ, ask Him. It is that simple.

I believe that many people never received the Spirit when they believed because they never even heard that there is a Holy Spirit. They had merely heard the gospel of repentance. They may have been led to feel sorry for their sins. They may have been baptized in water. They may have even gone through the motions of repeating a prayer asking for forgiveness and asking Jesus to come into their heart. But through this entire process, they never even heard that there was a Holy Spirit.

Since believing, they may have joined a church. They may have begun reading the Bible. They may have made vows about living for the Lord and ceasing from sin. Yet, instead of embarking on lives overflowing with love, joy, and peace, they have experienced lives of struggle and frustration. They continually try to be better. They try to please God. But they find they do not have the power or the ability to do it. They need the Holy Spirit!

Can someone be born again and not know it? Can someone's spirit be made alive by the Holy Spirit and not know it? Can someone become a new creation and not know it? Can someone be transferred from darkness to light and not know it?

If you have been born again, if the Holy Spirit has come to indwell you, you will know it. He makes all things new.

He empowers you. He teaches you. He comforts you. He equips you to hear the Lord and to obey His voice. He overflows in you with love for the brothers, with joy in the Lord, and with praise and worship of our Father in heaven. The Spirit will completely change your life.

If you are not living a victorious Christian life, if you did not receive the Holy Spirit when you believed, I encourage you to simply ask our Father who is in heaven and He will give the Holy Spirit to you. Be persistent, keep asking, keep seeking, keep knocking and the door will be opened to you. The Father will give the Holy Spirit to those who ask Him. We have Jesus' assurance on this. If we truly believe Jesus, we will believe His promise regarding the Father's faithfulness to give us the Holy Spirit.

Remember, God wants the best for us. He wants us to know everything that is ours in Christ. It is for this reason that He wants to give us His Holy Spirit, that we might be enabled to live holy lives to His praise and to His glory.

According to Scripture, there is one sin that is unforgivable, that is the sin of blaspheming the Holy Spirit (Mark 3:29). To blaspheme the Holy Spirit means to speak against the Holy Spirit, to defame it, to revile it, to disrespect it as unnecessary. The reason this sin is unforgivable is that it is impossible to be saved, to be born again, without the Holy Spirit.

You must desire the Holy Spirit. You must trust the Holy Spirit enough to ask to receive Him into your spirit. Who is this Holy Spirit? In order to trust the Holy Spirit, to desire the Holy Spirit, we must understand who He is and how He operates in the life of a believer.

Jesus says in John 14:16-18, "I will ask the Father, and He will give you another Helper, that He may be with you forever; that is the Spirit of Truth, whom the world cannot receive, because it does not see Him or know Him, but you know Him because He abides with you and will be in you. I will not leave you as orphans; I will come to you."

Who is this Spirit of Truth? Jesus tells His disciples, "You know him, for he lives with you and will be in you." Then He tells them that He will not leave them as orphans without help, but that He Himself would come to them.

Clearly Jesus is revealing to His disciples that He Himself would be coming as the Spirit of Truth to dwell within them. This is further evidenced by Paul in 2 Corinthians 3:16-18 where he writes, "Now the Lord is the Spirit, and where the Spirit of the Lord is, there is liberty. But we all, with unveiled face, beholding as in a mirror the glory of the Lord, are being transformed into the same image from glory to glory, just as from the Lord, the Spirit." The "Lord" in this passage refers to Jesus Christ our Lord, and the "Spirit" refers to the Holy Spirit.

In John 7:37-39 Jesus said, "If anyone is thirsty, let him come to Me and drink. He who believes in Me, as the Scripture said, 'From his innermost being will flow rivers of living water.' But this He spoke of the Spirit, whom those who believed in Him were to receive; for the Spirit was not yet given, because Jesus was not yet glorified."

On the day of Pentecost, the Holy Spirit was poured out because Jesus had been glorified. Peter said in Acts 2:32-33, "This Jesus God raised up again, to which we are all witnesses. Therefore having been exalted to the right hand of God, and having received from the Father the promise of the Holy Spirit, He has poured forth this which you both see and hear." Jesus had been glorified, exalted to the right hand of the Father in heaven and thus the Holy Spirit could be poured out.

Jesus prayed to the Father in John 17:20-23, "I do not ask on behalf of these alone, but for those also who believe in Me through their word; that they may all be one; even as You, Father, are in Me and I in You, that they also may be in Us, so that the world may believe that You sent Me. The glory which You have given Me I have given to them, that they may be one, just as We are one; I in them and You in Me, that they may be perfected in unity, so that the world may know that You sent Me, and loved them, even as You have loved Me."

Jesus was not praying just for the twelve disciples, but for us who would believe through their word. He was praying for us, that we would be perfected in unity, so the world would know that He was indeed sent by the Father.

The indwelling Holy Spirit transmits to us the reality of all that Christ experienced in His life, death and resurrection and makes it our experience as we grow in Christ. The Spirit does this by teaching us, by revealing to us everything that is ours in Christ (I Corinthians 2:10-12).

In Christ, our sins are forgiven, and our consciences are cleansed (Colossians 1:14, Hebrews 9:14). In Christ, we are crucified with Him and buried with Him in the likeness of His death that we should no longer be slaves of sin, for he who has died is freed from sin.

Now we are empowered by the indwelling Spirit to present ourselves to God as being alive from the dead, and our members as instruments of righteousness to God. Having been set free from sin, we have become slaves of God, and we have our fruit unto holiness, and the end everlasting life (Romans 6:4-13, 22).

The law of the Spirit of life in Christ Jesus has set us free from the law of sin and of death (Romans 8:2). Now, when we walk by the leading of the Holy Spirit, we do not fulfill the lusts of the flesh, but instead, we love the brothers and glorify God (Galatians 5:16, I John 4:7-16). In the Spirit of the glorified Jesus, we are given everything we need to live holy, godly lives, fully pleasing to the Father (2 Peter 1:3).

"We are more than victorious through Him who loved us" (Romans 8:37, HCSB).

Chapter 2 Discussion Questions: Receiving the Holy Spirit

1. Why did Paul ask the disciples at Ephesus if they had received the Holy Spirit when they believed?
2. Why must our consciences be cleansed?
3. Why must we be set free from the dominion of sin in our lives?
4. What is required for us to be genuine Christians?
5. How can we receive the Holy Spirit?
6. Why does the Father want to give us the Holy Spirit?
7. Can someone be born again and not know it?
8. What is the unforgivable sin?
9. Why is this sin unforgivable?
10. Who is the Holy Spirit?
11. How is the reality of all that Christ experienced in His life, death, and resurrection transmitted to us?
12. What sets us free from the law of sin and of death?

SEPARATION FROM GOD

Genesis 2 records the account of God's creation of man, and how God took the man and placed him in the garden of Eden to care for it. In Genesis 2:7 we read, "Then the Lord God formed man of dust from the ground, and breathed into his nostrils the breath of life; and man became a living being." Verse 15 continues, "Then the Lord God took the man and put him into the garden of Eden to cultivate it and keep it."

God told the man that he could eat fruit from every tree of the garden. However, he was not to eat the fruit from the tree of the knowledge of good and evil or he would die. Verses 16-18 tell us, "The Lord God commanded the man, saying, 'From any tree of the garden you may eat freely; but from the tree of the knowledge of good and evil you shall not eat, for in the day that you eat from it you will surely die.'

"Then the Lord God said, 'It is not good for the man to be alone; I will make him a helper suitable for him.'" Because it was not good for man to be alone, God built a woman from the rib he had taken from the man. Then God brought the woman to the man. Chapter 2 ends with verse

25 telling us, "And the man and his wife were both naked and were not ashamed."

Genesis chapter 3 begins with the serpent, Satan, coming to the woman and questioning her about what God had said. The woman answers the serpent, "From the fruit of the trees of the garden we may eat; but from the fruit of the tree which is in the middle of the garden, God has said, 'You shall not eat from it or touch it, or you will die'" (Genesis 3:2-3).

The woman responds to the serpent, but incorrectly quotes what God had said about the tree of knowledge of good and evil. There is no record in Scripture of God telling either the man or the woman that if they touch it they would die. God told Adam, the man, about the tree of knowledge of good and evil in the midst of the garden in Genesis 2:16-17, while man was still alone. The woman may not have heard it directly from God, but perhaps only secondhand, from her husband.

"The serpent said to the woman, 'You surely will not die! For God knows that in the day you eat from it your eyes will be opened, and you will be like God, knowing good and evil'" (Genesis 3:4-5). It was the serpent's contention that God was not a good God and that He was withholding the best from Adam and his wife, Eve.

Being deceived by the serpent, Eve began to see that the fruit of the tree of knowledge of good and evil was good to eat, a delight to look at, and very desirable to make one wise. So she touched it. Nothing happened. So she ate of it and gave some to her husband, Adam, and he ate of it.

Immediately upon rebelling against God by disobeying His command not to eat from the tree of the knowledge of good and evil, the eyes of Adam and his wife were opened, and they knew they were naked. Mankind now had received an inner innate knowledge of good and evil. This knowledge made them aware of their nakedness, and they were ashamed.

They sewed fig leaves (vegetation) together to try to cover their nakedness. But when they became aware of God's presence, the covering of vegetation didn't help. They still felt ashamed and felt naked before God. Because of their shame and their sense of guilt, they were afraid and tried to hide from God's presence.

Genesis 3:9-13 says, "Then the LORD God called to the man and said to him, 'Where are you?' He said, 'I heard the sound of You in the garden, and I was afraid because I was naked; so I hid myself.' And He said, 'Who told you that you were naked? Have you eaten from the tree of which I commanded you not to eat?' The man said, 'The woman whom You gave to be with me, she gave me from the tree, and I ate.' Then the LORD God said to the woman, 'What is this you have done?' And the woman said, 'The serpent deceived me, and I ate.'"

Then God cursed the serpent because he had deceived the woman. He said to the serpent in Genesis 3:15, "And I will put enmity between thee and the woman, and between thy seed and her seed; it shall bruise thy head, and thou shalt bruise his heel" (KJV). This statement by God to the serpent, Satan, the devil, is one of the most extraordinary passages in all of Scripture. God is revealing something of His plan to use the seed of the woman to destroy the serpent, Satan. Few verses in Scripture contain a greater promise or more hope than this verse! In the midst of overwhelming darkness and despair, God provides a ray of light, a glimmer of hope.

After confessing their sin of rebellion and disobedience, God passes judgment on Adam and Eve. He tells them that their lives would become painful and full of hard labor. Even though their confession was filled with excuses, God had mercy on them and made garments of animal skins and clothed them both, covering their nakedness. This process of making the garments required that animals be killed and their blood shed. By shedding this blood to cover the guilt and shame of their sins, God has revealed to man what He requires for man's atonement, for sins to be forgiven, so that man might, at least outwardly, be at peace with God.

Hebrews 9:22 says, "And according to the Law, one may almost say, all things are cleansed with blood, and without shedding of blood there is no forgiveness." Even though their sins are confessed and covered through the shedding of blood, disobedience often carries a heavy price.

Genesis 3 ends with verses 22-24 telling us that "God said, 'Behold, the man has become like one of Us, knowing good and evil; and now, he might stretch out his hand, and take also from the tree of life, and eat, and live forever'— therefore the LORD God sent him out from the garden of Eden, to cultivate the ground from which he was taken. So He drove the man out; and at the east of the garden of Eden He stationed the cherubim and the flaming sword which turned every direction to guard the way to the tree of life."

Adam sinned. He disobeyed God. Therefore, God put man out of the garden to keep him from eating from the tree of life. He drove man away from His presence to prevent man from eating from the tree and receiving eternal life that he might live forever. Man's sin resulted in him being separated from God. It also resulted in his life being transformed from one of fellowship with God, enjoying

God's abundant provision for his every need, to a life of hardship, suffering, sin, guilt, and death.

As a consequence of sin, man was driven out of God's kingdom of life, light, and peace, and into Satan's kingdom of this world; a kingdom of darkness, death, and fear. Hebrews 2:14 tells us that Jesus, the seed of the woman, became flesh and blood, "that through death He might render powerless him who had the power of death, that is, the devil, and might free those who through fear of death were subject to slavery all their lives."

Man's disobedience had made him a slave to sin. Paul writes in Romans 6:16, "Do you not know that when you present yourselves to someone as slaves for obedience, you are slaves of the one whom you obey, either of sin resulting in death, or of obedience resulting in righteousness?"

Paul tells us in Romans 5:18, "Through one transgression there resulted condemnation to all men." He continues in verse 19, "Through the one man's disobedience the many were made sinners." These verses reveal that through Adam's one transgression, through his one act of disobedience, condemnation resulted to all men, and that all were made sinners.

By Adam's one act of rebellion and disobedience, we were all constituted as sinners. We were made sinners because through Adam's one act, the nature of mankind was changed. Our nature was transformed in the moment of disobedience from innocence to sinfulness. We now sin because we are sinners by nature. There is a thing within us that is not good. It is this sin within us that causes us to sin. The sin within us causes us to do the things that we don't want to do. Mankind has become slaves to sin.

In Romans 7, Paul explains perfectly the experience of the sinner, of the unregenerate man. In Romans 7:14-24

Paul writes, "For we know that the Law is spiritual, but I am of flesh, sold into bondage to sin. For what I am doing, I do not understand; for I am not practicing what I would like to do, but I am doing the very thing I hate. But if I do the very thing I do not want to do, I agree with the Law, confessing that the Law is good.

"So now, no longer am I the one doing it, but sin which dwells in me. For I know that nothing good dwells in me, that is, in my flesh; for the willing is present in me, but the doing of the good is not. For the good that I want, I do not do, but I practice the very evil that I do not want. But if I am doing the very thing I do not want, I am no longer the one doing it, but sin which dwells in me.

"I find then the principle that evil is present in me, the one who wants to do good. For I joyfully concur with the law of God in the inner man, but I see a different law in the members of my body, waging war against the law of my mind and making me a prisoner of the law of sin which is in my members." Because man is now enslaved to sin, dominated by it, he finds himself doing things that he does not want to do. Sin in the flesh has taken dominion over man.

Satan, the serpent, had gained what was apparently a huge victory. Through his deception of the woman, he had caused man to sin, to rebel against the God that created them. Man was now in the world, in Satan's kingdom of darkness and under the power of the evil one. I John 5:19 confirms this saying, "The whole world lies in the power of the evil one."

In Genesis 4, we see that Adam had passed the lesson of the shedding of blood down to his sons. One son obeyed and followed the teaching about the shedding of blood, but the other son rebelled and tried to appease God by his own efforts according to his own understanding.

"In the course of time Cain presented some of the land's produce as an offering to the LORD. And Abel also presented an offering—some of the firstborn of his flock and their fat portions. The LORD had regard for Abel and his offering, but He did not have regard for Cain and his offering. Cain was furious, and he looked despondent.

"Then the LORD said to Cain, 'Why are you furious? And why do you look despondent? If you do what is right, won't you be accepted? But if you do not do what is right, sin is crouching at the door. Its desire is for you, but you must rule over it'" (Genesis 4:3-7).

Cain brought an offering of vegetation to the Lord. Abel brought the firstlings of his flock and their fat portions. God accepted Abel's sacrifice because it honored God by acknowledging the need for the shedding of blood for sins to be forgiven. Cain's offering showed no acknowledgement of sins or of the need for a blood sacrifice. Because Cain saw nothing wrong with his offering, he believed that God had treated him unjustly, and became angry. In anger, he rose up and killed his brother. Cain's refusal to acknowledge the sin that was crouching at his door, prevented him from mastering it.

From the first four chapters of Genesis, it has become clear that mankind has two very serious problems that keep him separated from God and prevent him from having any permanent peace with God. First, there is the problem of the sins that he commits. These sins, like Adam's sin, separate him from the presence of the righteous and holy God, and prevent man from partaking of God's eternal life. These sins also defile man's conscience, preventing him from having any real peace with God.

Second, there is the problem of the sin nature that dwells within the heart of mankind. It has enslaved him. It dominates his will and causes him to sin. Even if something can be done to atone for the sins that man commits, he still continues to sin because he has become constituted a sinner by nature. The sin nature within us has dominion over us and causes us to do what we don't want to do. It causes us to sin! However, through the promised seed of the woman that God spoke of in Genesis 3:15, God would fully address each of these problems.

Chapter 3 Discussion Questions: Separation from God

1. What tree in the garden of Eden did God tell man not to eat of?
2. What did God say would happen to man in the day that he eats of that tree?
3. What did God say would happen to man if he touched the fruit of that tree?
4. Why is it important to hear God speaking directly to us and not just hear things second hand?
5. The woman was deceived, but why did the man eat the forbidden fruit?
6. Why did Adam and Eve try to cover themselves with the fig leaves?
7. What promise did God make in Genesis 3:15?
8. What process did God go through to cover their nakedness? Why?
9. What is the significance of the shedding of blood?
10. Why did God block the way to the tree of life?
11. What was the consequence of man's sin?
12. How did man's nature change as a result of his disobedience?

13. How do we know that Paul is speaking of the experience of the sinner, the unregenerate man in Romans 7?

14. What two problems keep man separated from God and prevent him from having any permanent peace with God?

RECONCILIATION AND FREEDOM

God begins the process of fulfilling His promise concerning the seed of the woman by choosing a people for Himself. The whole world is in sin and darkness, but God calls a man to come out of the world unto Himself.

"Now the LORD had said unto Abram, 'Get thee out of thy country, and from thy kindred, and from thy father's house, unto a land that I will shew thee: And I will make of thee a great nation, and I will bless thee, and make thy name great; and thou shalt be a blessing: And I will bless them that bless thee, and curse him that curseth thee: and in thee shall all families of the earth be blessed.' So Abram departed, as the LORD had spoken unto him; and Lot went with him: and Abram was seventy and five years old when he departed out of Haran" (Genesis 12:1-4, KJV).

In Genesis 15:1-6, the word of the Lord came to Abram, reinforcing this promise, telling him that his seed would be as numerous as the stars in the sky. God "took him outside and said, 'Look up at the sky and count the stars—if indeed you can count them.' Then he said to him, 'So shall your offspring be.' Abram believed the LORD, and he credited it to him as righteousness."

At that time Abram had no offspring, yet he believed God, and it was credited to him as righteousness. God began to reveal to Abram how His promise concerning the seed of the woman would be fulfilled. Then in Genesis 17, God appeared to Abram again and changed his name to Abraham, because God said He would make him a father of many nations. Then in verse 8, God promised him, "And I will give unto thee, and to thy seed after thee, the land wherein thou art a stranger, all the land of Canaan, for an everlasting possession; and I will be their God" (KJV).

Paul explains to us in Galatians 3:16-18 who this "seed" is. He writes, "Now the promises were spoken to Abraham and to his seed. He does not say, 'And to seeds,' as referring to many, but rather to one, 'And to your seed,' that is, Christ. What I am saying is this: the Law, which came four hundred and thirty years later, does not invalidate a covenant previously ratified by God, so as to nullify the promise. For if the inheritance is based on law, it is no longer based on a promise; but God has granted it to Abraham by means of a promise."

The Law was given as a school master, a tutor, to preserve God's people until the promise of faith arrived. Galatians 3:23-24 says, "Before faith came, we were kept in custody under the law, being shut up to the faith which was later to be revealed. Therefore the Law has become our tutor to lead us to Christ, so that we may be justified by faith."

Galatians 4:3-5 says, "While we were children, we were held in bondage under the elemental things of the world. But when the fullness of the time came, God sent forth His Son, born of a woman, born under the Law, so that He might redeem those who were under the Law, that we might receive the adoption as sons."

When God gave the Law through Moses under the first covenant, He established offerings whereby the priest could make atonement for the people so their sins could be forgiven. Leviticus 4 tells us that the person who has sinned is to bring his sin offering to the priest. The sinner is to lay his hand on the head of the sin offering before the Lord. The offering is killed and the priest is to take some of the blood of the offering and apply it to the horns of the altar of the burnt offering. Verse 26 says, "In this way the priest will make atonement on his behalf for that person's sin, and he will be forgiven."

Under the law, God provided a process through the shedding of the blood of bulls and goats that the priests could make atonement for themselves and for the people, and their sins would be forgiven. Through this covering of their sins, the Israelites would be considered by God to be clean ceremonially, outwardly, and worthy to join in the fellowship of the assembly of His people. By the offerings of the Law under the first covenant, God's people were reminded, that without the shedding of blood, there is no forgiveness of sins.

Hebrews 10:1-4 says, "For the Law, since it has only a shadow of the good things to come and not the very form of things, can never, by the same sacrifices which they offer continually year by year, make perfect those who draw near. Otherwise, would they not have ceased to be offered, because the worshipers, having once been cleansed, would no longer have had consciousness of sins? But in those sacrifices there is a reminder of sins year by year. For it is impossible for the blood of bulls and goats to take away sins."

Christ fulfilled the Law. Jesus said in Matthew 5:17, "Do not think that I came to abolish the Law or the

Prophets; I did not come to abolish but to fulfill." In the new covenant He is writing the Laws on our hearts. He accomplishes this by the Holy Spirit that the Father gives to live within us. This Spirit teaches us all things that are ours in Christ.

The word translated "Law" in the Old Testament, "Torah," comes from the root word "yara." Yara means to point out, to teach, to instruct. The Law was given to teach us about God and His ways. Under the new covenant, the Holy Spirit is given to us by the Father to do just that. However, this Spirit not only teaches us, but also empowers us to live according to His teaching and instruction. The new covenant is not weak through the flesh, but strong through the Spirit working within the believer.

The Law has not changed. The Laws that God is writing on our hearts are the same Laws He gave to Moses in Exodus 24. In verse 12, the Lord said to Moses, "Come up to Me on the mountain and remain there, and I will give you the stone tablets with the law and the commandment which I have written for their instruction."

In Matthew 22:37-40, when asked which is the greatest commandment in the Law, Jesus said, "'Love the Lord your God with all your heart and with all your soul and with all your mind.' This is the first and greatest commandment. And the second is like it: 'Love your neighbor as yourself.' All the Law and the Prophets hang on these two commandments" (NIV). Romans 5:5 says, "The love of God has been poured out within our hearts through the Holy Spirit who was given to us." This love of God is writing these Laws on our hearts by the Holy Spirit, and by that same Spirit He is empowering us to fulfill these Laws as we are led by the Spirit.

However, the process for fulfilling the Law has changed. The process has changed from the weakness of the flesh to the strength of the Spirit, and from works of the flesh to faith in Christ Jesus. "Man is not justified by the works of the Law but through faith in Christ Jesus" (Galatians 2:16). "It is not the children of the flesh who are children of God, but the children of the promise are regarded as descendants" (Romans 9:8). Those that, like Abraham, by faith believe the promise, are God's children. Their faith is credited to them as righteousness.

"For what the Law could not do, weak as it was through the flesh, God did: sending His own Son in the likeness of sinful flesh and as an offering for sin, He condemned sin in the flesh" (Romans 8:3). Let us summarize some of the things that the Law could not do, that God did through His Son Jesus Christ our Lord, the seed of the woman.

The offerings and sacrifices of the first covenant could not take away sins. Hebrews 10:11 says, "Every priest stands daily ministering and offering time after time the same sacrifices, which can never take away sins." It is recorded in John 1:29 that John the Baptist saw Jesus coming unto him and said, "Behold the Lamb of God, which taketh away the sin of the world" (KJV). I John 3:5 tells us that Christ appeared "in order to take away sins." In promising to make a new covenant with His people, God says, "And this is my covenant with them when I take away their sins" (Romans 11:27).

The Law could not cleanse the conscience of the people. Hebrews 9:9 states that under the first covenant, "Gifts and sacrifices are offered which cannot make the worshiper perfect in conscience." Therefore, God sent His own Son, the seed of the woman, to cleanse the conscience of the people. "For if the blood of goats and bulls and the ashes of a heifer sprinkling those who have been defiled sanctify for the cleansing of the flesh, how much more will the blood of Christ, who through the eternal Spirit offered Himself without blemish to God, cleanse your conscience" (Hebrews 9:13-14). The sprinkling of the blood of bulls and goats could only sanctify for the cleansing of the flesh, but the blood of Christ cleanses the conscience.

With the first covenant, under the Law, sins could be atoned for and forgiven, but they could never be taken away. Therefore, the people always had a consciousness of sins. When a believer's sins are atoned for and forgiven by virtue of faith in Christ, the blood of Christ takes away that person's sins and cleanses their conscience. It is by this taking away of the sins and the cleansing of the conscience that the believer has peace with God.

If, upon confessing a sin and making restitution when instructed by the Spirit to do so, after the blood of Christ has taken away the sin and cleansed our conscience concerning it, our minds should no longer be troubled by thoughts of that sin. If accusing thoughts of that sin ever enter our minds, we need to understand that it is an attack of the enemy, Satan. We need to be strengthened and encouraged in our faith in Christ and His shed blood, and remember the words in Revelation 12:10-11, "The accuser of our brethren has been thrown down, he who accuses them before our God day and night. And they overcame him because of the blood of the Lamb and because of the word of their testimony."

When the enemy, the accuser, attacks, we need to turn our hearts and our minds to Christ and His faithfulness. We need to praise Him for His blood that has cleansed us and has taken away our sin. We need to turn the enemy's attacks into victorious praises to our God. We will soon find that the attacks will cease because they are unprofitable.

The Law could not make anything perfect. Hebrews 7:18-19, "The Law made nothing perfect." However, Hebrews 10:14 says, "For by one offering He (Christ) has perfected for all time those who are sanctified." The word "perfect" in these passages means "complete." The Law could only sanctify to the cleansing of the flesh. Its sanctification was only outward, it was not complete. The sanctification accomplished by the blood of Christ is complete, even to the cleansing of our conscience and the transforming of our soul by His life.

The works of the Law can justify no one. Paul writes in Galatians 2:16, "Knowing that a man is not justified by the works of the Law but through faith in Christ Jesus, even we have believed in Christ Jesus, so that we may be justified by faith in Christ and not by the works of the Law; since by the works of the Law no flesh will be justified." Romans 5:9 tells us that we are "justified by His blood." The blood of Christ justifies the believer. The Law never can.

The Law could not give life. "Is the Law then contrary to the promises of God? May it never be! For if a law had been given which was able to impart life, then righteousness would indeed have been based on law" (Galatians 3:21). Jesus said in John 10:10, "I came that they may have life, and have it abundantly." Paul writes in Romans 5:9-10, "Much more then, having now been justified by His blood, we shall be saved from the wrath of God through Him. For if while we were enemies we were reconciled to God through the death of His Son, much more, having been reconciled, we shall be saved by His life." Finally, John writes in I John 5:12, "He who has the Son has the life; he who does not have the Son of God does not have the life."

The Law cannot free us from bondage to sin. "For sin shall not be master over you, for you are not under the law but under grace" (Romans 6:14). When we were under the Law, sin was our master. However, Paul tells us that we need to understand, "that our old self was crucified with Him (with Christ) in order that sin's dominion over the body may be abolished, so that we may no longer be enslaved to sin, since a person who has died is freed from sin's claims" (Romans 6:6-7, HCSB).

It was because these things could not be accomplished by the Law that the process had to be changed. "For if there had been nothing wrong with that first covenant, no place would have been sought for another. But God found fault with the people and said: 'The days are coming, declares the Lord, when I will make a new covenant with the people of Israel and with the people of Judah'" (Hebrews 8:7-8). Verse 13 continues, "When He said, 'A new covenant,' He has made the first obsolete. But whatever is becoming obsolete and growing old is ready to disappear."

In changing the process, God did through Jesus Christ, the seed of the woman, what the Law could not do. We are told in Hebrews 9:15, it is for this reason that, "He (Christ) is the mediator of a new covenant, so that, since a death has taken place for the redemption of the transgressions that were committed under the first covenant, those who have been called may receive the promise of the eternal inheritance." Hebrews 7:23-25, "The former priests, on the one hand, existed in greater numbers because they were prevented by death from continuing, but Jesus, on the other hand, because He continues forever, holds His priesthood permanently.

"Therefore, He is able also to save forever those who draw near to God through Him, since He always lives to make intercession for them." "But now He has obtained a more excellent ministry, by as much as He is also the mediator of a better covenant, which has been enacted on better promises" (Hebrews 8:6).

In this new covenant, because of the value that God has placed on the blood of Christ, we can draw near to God with boldness and confidence. We need to value the blood of Christ because God values the blood of Christ. Hebrews 10:19 and 22, says, "Since we have confidence to enter the holy place by the blood of Jesus. Let us draw near with a sincere heart in full assurance of faith, having our hearts sprinkled clean from an evil conscience."

There are two crucial aspects of the victory that Christ has gained for us; the shedding of the blood and the seed of the woman bruising the head of the serpent. When God established the Passover, He gave the children of Israel specific instructions about killing an unblemished year-old lamb, eating it, and applying the blood so that the angel of death would pass over them and not harm them. Exodus 12:13 says, "And the blood shall be to you for a token upon the houses where ye are: and when I see the blood, I will pass over you, and the plague shall not be upon you to destroy you, when I smite the land of Egypt" (KJV).

God told them, "When I see the blood, I will pass over you." God looked at Abel and saw that he trusted in the shedding of the blood. God looked at the children of Israel at the Passover and saw that they trusted in the shedding of the blood. God looked at those under the Law of the first covenant and saw that they were trusting the blood. Today God looks at us to see if we are trusting in the blood that was shed when Jesus offered Himself as a sacrifice for our sins.

When God saw the blood applied by faith to the door posts and lentils, He passed over them and they were not harmed by the angel of death. When God looks at us today, He looks to see if our faith is in Christ and in the blood he shed for us.

The other crucial aspect of the salvation that we have in Christ is the bruising of the head of the serpent. Christ's death on the cross accomplished this. That is why Paul writes in I Corinthians 1:18, "For the word of the cross is foolishness to those who are perishing, but to us who are being saved it is the power of God." Then in Colossians 1:18-19 Paul writes, "For it was the Father's good pleasure for all the fullness to dwell in Him, and through Him to reconcile all things to Himself, having made peace through the blood of His cross."

Everything that the serpent accomplished in causing man to sin and destroying the peace and the fellowship between God and man, Christ destroyed by His death on the cross. By His death on the cross, Christ took away our sins and broke the power of sin over us. He reconciled us to God having made peace through the blood of His cross.

Under the Law, God's people were always subject to slavery to sin. No matter how zealous they were for God, no matter how hard they would try to please God and live holy lives, the sin nature within them would overpower them and cause them to sin. However, Hebrews 2:14-15 reveals that, "Since the children share in flesh and blood, He (Christ) Himself likewise also partook of the same, that through death He might render powerless him who had the power of death, that is, the devil, and might free those who through fear of death were subject to slavery all their lives." Christ bruised the head of the serpent, rendering him powerless to continue to hold us in bondage through fear of death. The power of the sin nature was broken. We were set free from the law of sin and of death.

Romans 8:2-4 confirms this, "For the law of the Spirit of life in Christ Jesus has set you free from the law of sin and of death. For what the Law could not do, weak as it was through the flesh, God did: sending His own Son in the likeness of sinful flesh and as an offering for sin, He condemned sin in the flesh, so that the requirement of the Law might be fulfilled in us, who do not walk according to the flesh but according to the Spirit." When Christ was crucified, God placed us together in Him. That is why Paul says that we were crucified with Christ.

Paul reminds us in Romans 6:2-7, "How shall we who died to sin still live in it? Or do you not know that all of us who have been baptized into Christ Jesus have been baptized into His death? Therefore we have been buried with Him through baptism into death, so that as Christ was raised from the dead through the glory of the Father, so we too might walk in newness of life. For if we have become united with Him in the likeness of His death, certainly we shall also be in the likeness of His resurrection, knowing this, that our old self was crucified with Him, in order that our body of sin might be done away with, so that we would no longer be slaves to sin; for he who has died is freed from sin."

The only way we can "know this" is by the Holy Spirit revealing it to us. Once the Holy Spirit reveals to us the truth, the reality, of our death with Christ, then we can go on to reckon or consider ourselves as dead to sin. Romans 6:11 says, "Even so consider yourselves to be dead to sin, but alive to God in Christ Jesus." We can consider ourselves dead to sin, we can reckon ourselves dead to sin all day long and still find no freedom from the bondage to sin until we know for a fact that we died with Christ. And we can only know the reality of our death with Christ if the Spirit reveals it to us.

When, by the Spirit's opening of our eyes, we see the reality of our death with Christ, we will no longer struggle to please God. We will realize that in ourselves we cannot please God. It is only as we look to Jesus, the author and finisher of our faith, can we please God by submitting to the leading of the Holy Spirit within us. Romans 8:7-9 confirms this saying, "because the mind set on the flesh is hostile toward God; for it does not subject itself to the law of God, for it is not even able to do so, and those who are in the flesh cannot please God. However, you are not in the flesh but in the Spirit, if indeed the Spirit of God dwells in you. But if anyone does not have the Spirit of Christ, he does not belong to Him."

Paul encourages us in Galatians 5:16, "Walk by the Spirit, and you will not carry out the desire of the flesh." 2 Peter 1:3-4 says, "His divine power has granted to us everything pertaining to life and godliness, through the true knowledge of Him who called us by His own glory and excellence. For by these He has granted to us His precious and magnificent promises, so that by them you may become partakers of the divine nature, having escaped the corruption that is in the world by lust."

As the seed of the woman bruising the serpent's head by shedding His blood for us on the cross, Christ has won a total and complete victory. "For it was fitting for us to have such a high priest, holy, innocent, undefiled, separated from sinners and exalted above the heavens; who does not need daily, like those high priests, to offer up sacrifices, first for His own sins and then for the sins of the people, because this He did once for all when He offered up Himself. For the Law appoints men as high priests who are weak, but the word of the oath, which came after the Law, appoints a Son, made perfect forever" (Hebrews 7:26-28).

"Now the main point in what has been said is this: we have such a high priest, who has taken His seat at the right hand of the throne of the Majesty in the heavens, a minister in the sanctuary and in the true tabernacle, which the Lord pitched, not man" (Hebrews 8:1-2). When we walk by the Spirit we are walking in the victory of Christ. When we walk by the Spirit, we truly are victorious Christians.

"Then I looked, and I heard the voice of many angels around the throne and the living creatures and the elders; and the number of them was myriads of myriads, and thousands of thousands, saying with a loud voice, 'Worthy is the Lamb that was slain to receive power and riches and wisdom and might and honor and glory and blessing.' And every created thing which is in heaven and on the earth and under the earth and on the sea, and all things in them, I heard saying, 'To Him who sits on the throne, and to the Lamb, be blessing and honor and glory and dominion forever and ever.' And the four living creatures kept saying, 'Amen.' And the elders fell down and worshiped."

May we worship the Lord by walking by the Spirit, not fulfilling the lusts of the flesh. When we walk by the Spirit, and not by the flesh, we are holy, and we are wholly pleasing to God. By the blood and by the cross, we are reconciled to God, and we are freed from sin's dominion to walk in the newness of Christ's life within us. Then we are victorious!

Chapter 4 Discussion Questions: Reconciliation and Freedom

1. Why did God call Abram?
2. What did God promise Abram?
3. What did Abram do in response to God's promise?
4. How did God react to Abram's response?
5. Who is the promised seed of the woman?
6. How was the Law changed from the first covenant to the new covenant?
7. How was the process of keeping the Law changed?
8. What six things could the Law not do, that God did through His Son Jesus?
9. Why could the Law not do these things?
10. Why do we need to value the blood of Christ?
11. On what basis do we have boldness and confidence to draw near to God?
12. How are we set free from the dominion of sin?
13. When are we truly victorious Christians?

UNDERSTANDING SALVATION

Many people think of salvation only in terms of either being saved or being lost. To be saved, for many people, means to go to heaven when you die. To be lost, for many, means spending eternity in the fiery torments of hell.

Let us take some time to see what the Scriptures say about salvation. The Greek word translated as "saved" in the New Testament is sozo. Sozo or "saved" literally means "delivered" or "protected." To be saved or delivered can have many different applications.

Joel 2:32 says, "And it will come about that whoever calls on the name of the LORD will be delivered." The word "call" here means to cry out as someone would cry out for help when trapped in a burning building with no evident way of escape. This is not a casual or pointless, vain, calling on the name of the Lord. It is a screaming desperation of a soul crying out for help, for deliverance from a seemingly hopeless situation.

What God has promised, He will do. God will faithfully deliver that person from his situation of distress. Psalm 34:4 says, "I sought the LORD, and He answered me, and delivered me from all my fears." Psalm 107:6, 13, 19, 28 assures us of God's faithfulness, "Then they cried out to the LORD in their trouble; He delivered them out of their distresses." These were people fainting from hunger and thirst, prisoners in misery and chains, people that were near the gates of death, sailors whose souls melted away in their misery as storms ravaged them upon the waves of the sea.

In each circumstance, they cried out and God delivered them from their distress. This deliverance does not, however, mean that they are saved eternally. It is simply God's faithfulness to deliver, or save, those that, in their distress, cry out to Him for help. This is a temporal deliverance, or salvation.

Sozo, or saved, has another application. This is one of eternal salvation. Titus 3:4-7 says, "When the kindness of God our Savior and His love for mankind appeared, He saved us, not on the basis of deeds which we have done in righteousness, but according to His mercy, by the washing of regeneration and renewing by the Holy Spirit, whom He poured out upon us richly through Jesus Christ our Savior, so that being justified by His grace we would be made heirs according to the hope of eternal life." Notice that Paul says that believers have been saved (past tense) by the renewing of the Holy Spirit. By this renewing, this being born of the Spirit, they have the hope of eternal life.

John 3:5-7 says, "Jesus answered, 'Truly, truly, I say to you, unless one is born of water and the Spirit he cannot enter into the kingdom of God. That which is born of the flesh is flesh, and that which is born of the Spirit is spirit. Do not be amazed that I said to you, 'You must be born again.''' We are made alive by being born again. We are saved, born again, when the Holy Spirit quickens, or gives life, to our spirit.

Romans 10:8-13 says, "that is, the word of faith which we are preaching, that if you confess with your mouth Jesus as Lord, and believe in your heart that God raised Him from the dead, you will be saved; for with the heart a person believes, resulting in righteousness, and with the mouth he confesses, resulting in salvation. For the Scripture says, "WHOEVER BELIEVES IN HIM WILL NOT BE DISAPPOINTED." For there is no distinction between Jew and Greek; for the same Lord is Lord of all, abounding in riches for all who call on Him; for "WHOEVER WILL CALL ON THE NAME OF THE LORD WILL BE SAVED." The Lord is rich to all who by faith in Jesus call on His name, believing that God has raised Him from the dead.

This is the salvation of our spirit. We are made alive by the life-giving Spirit of Christ entering into our spirit. We are now able, by faith, to have fellowship with God through our Lord Jesus Christ. He has made us alive spiritually. Our spirit has been saved.

When Jesus, as the Spirit of Truth, comes to indwell our spirit, He makes us alive to God. He becomes our life and has promised that he will never leave us (Hebrews 13:5). We have been saved by this salvation of our spirit. This aspect of eternal salvation is completed when our spirit is born of the Holy Spirit.

This, however, is not the end of the salvation process. It is just the beginning. When we are born again, our spirit is made alive; we have been saved. We now embark on the next phase of the salvation process, the salvation of our soul.

Now the Lord begins to work within us to transform us, to change our desires, how we think, and talk, and act. God begins the life-long process of conforming us to His image. "For those whom He foreknew, He also predestined to become conformed to the image of His Son" (Romans 8:29). 2 Corinthians 3:18 says, "We all, with unveiled face, beholding as in a mirror the glory of the Lord, are being transformed into the same image from glory to glory, just as from the Lord, the Spirit."

He accomplishes this purpose of transformation, of conformation, by teaching us to hear His voice and to obey His speaking as we look to Him and submit to Him as Lord. Jesus says in John 10:1-4, "Truly, truly, I say to you, he who does not enter by the door into the fold of the sheep, but climbs up some other way, he is a thief and a robber. But he who enters by the door is the shepherd of the sheep. To him the doorkeeper opens, and the sheep hear his voice, and he calls his own sheep by name and leads them out. When he puts forth all his own, he goes ahead of them, and the sheep follow him because they know his voice." Verses 15-16 say, "I lay down My life for the sheep. I have other sheep, which are not of this fold; I must bring them also, and they will hear My voice; and they will become one flock with one shepherd."

He teaches us to joyfully submit to His will. Romans 12:1-2 says, "Therefore I urge you, brethren, by the mercies of God, to present your bodies a living and holy sacrifice, acceptable to God, which is your spiritual service of worship. And do not be conformed to this world, but be transformed by the renewing of your mind, so that you may prove what the will of God is, that which is good and acceptable and perfect." He uses many circumstances, many situations, to help us to learn how much God loves us and how God wants the best for us. He teaches us that apart from Him we can do nothing, but through Him we can do all things. (John 15:5; Philippians 4:13)

He brings us through trials to test and purify our faith which is more precious than gold. "Blessed be the God and Father of our Lord Jesus Christ, who according to his great mercy caused us to be born again to a living hope through the resurrection of Jesus Christ from the dead, to an incorruptible and undefiled inheritance that doesn't fade away, reserved in Heaven for you, who by the power of God are guarded through faith for a salvation ready to be revealed in the last time. Wherein you greatly rejoice, though now for a little while, if need be, you have been grieved in various trials, that the proof of your faith, which is more precious than gold that perishes even though it is tested by fire, may be found to result in praise, glory, and honor at the revelation of Jesus Christ—whom, not having known, you love. In him, though now you don't see him, yet believing, you rejoice greatly with joy that is unspeakable and full of glory, receiving the result of your faith, the salvation of your souls" (I Peter 1:3-9, WEB).

He uses trials to teach us obedience through suffering and to bring us to maturity. "Dear friends, do not be surprised at the fiery ordeal that has come on you to test you, as though something strange were happening to you. But rejoice inasmuch as you participate in the sufferings of Christ, so that you may be overjoyed when his glory is revealed" (I Peter 4:12-13, NIV). Jesus, "in the days of his flesh, having offered up prayers and petitions with strong crying and tears to him who was able to save him from death, and having been heard for his godly fear, though he was a Son, yet learned obedience by the things which he suffered. Having been made perfect, he became to all of those who obey him the author of eternal salvation" (Hebrews 5:7-9, WEB). In the same way, we learn obedience through suffering and are brought on to maturity, perfection, through the things that we suffer for the Lord's sake.

He renews our minds that we would think on things that are just, and pure, and righteous. Philippians 4:8 says, "Finally, brethren, whatever is true, whatever is honorable, whatever is right, whatever is pure, whatever is lovely, whatever is of good repute, if there is any excellence and if anything worthy of praise, dwell on these things. The things you have learned and received and heard and seen in me, practice these things, and the God of peace will be with you."

He trains our minds to see things according to the Spirit and not according to the flesh. "You were taught, with regard to your former way of life, to put off your old self, which is being corrupted by its deceitful desires; to be made new in the attitude of your minds; and to put on the new self, created to be like God in true righteousness and holiness" (Ephesians 4:22-24, NIV).

He pours out His love in our hearts that we might love one another as He first loved us. Romans 5:5 says, "The love of God has been poured out within our hearts through the Holy Spirit who was given to us." Jesus said in John 13:34-35, "A new commandment I give to you, that you love one another, even as I have loved you, that you also love one another. By this all men will know that you are My disciples, if you have love for one another." It is by the empowering of the indwelling Holy Spirit through which the love of God has been poured out in our hearts that we are enabled to keep this commandment.

He teaches us to humble ourselves and to cast all our cares upon Him as we learn how much He cares for us. "All of you be subject one to another, and be clothed with humility: for God resisteth the proud, and giveth grace to the humble. Humble yourselves therefore under the mighty hand of God, that he may exalt you in due time: Casting all your care upon him; for he careth for you" (I Peter 5:5-7, KJV). He teaches us to be anxious for nothing, but to rest in Him and His righteousness.

Jesus gives us peace that surpasses all understanding as we begin to realize, through experience and through the Scriptures, that He is our peace, that it is by His blood alone that we have peace with God. "He is our peace. He came and preached peace to you who were far off and to those who were near. For through him we both have our access in one Spirit to the Father" (Ephesians 2:14, 17-18, WEB). Philippians 4:7 says, "The peace of God, which surpasses all comprehension, will guard your hearts and your minds in Christ Jesus." Jesus said, "I will never leave thee, nor forsake thee" (Hebrews 13:5, KJV).

The more readily and the more completely we submit to His will, to His life working in us, looking away to Him, the more completely we begin to experience the reality of our death with Him and the complete deliverance that He gives us from the dominion and power of sin in our lives. Romans 6:2-7 says, "How shall we who died to sin still live in it? Or do you not know that all of us who have been baptized into Christ Jesus have been baptized into His death? Therefore we have been buried with Him through baptism into death, so that as Christ was raised from the dead through the glory of the Father, so we too might walk in newness of life. For if we have become united with Him in the likeness of His death, certainly we shall also be in the likeness of His resurrection, knowing this, that our old self was crucified with Him, in order that our body of sin might be done away with, so that we would no longer be slaves to sin; for he who has died is freed from sin."

Once we know our death with Christ and begin to reckon our freedom from the dominion of sin in our body, the more completely we begin to experience the unspeakable joy of living a holy life, wholly pleasing to God, empowered by His indestructible life working in us according to His vast power. Paul writes, "I pray that the perception of your mind may be enlightened so you may know what is the hope of His calling, what are the glorious riches of His inheritance among the saints, and what is the immeasurable greatness of His power to us who believe, according to the working of His vast strength" (Ephesians 1:18-19, HCSB).

This life-long process is the salvation of the soul. The completion of this process is the goal of our faith. "You believe in Him and rejoice with inexpressible and glorious joy, because you are receiving the goal of your faith, the salvation of your souls" (I Peter 1:8-9, HCSB).

The extent to which this process is completed will determine the glory of Christ that we will each enjoy in the resurrection. In the resurrection each believer will differ in glory, just as each star in the sky differs from one another in glory. The amount of glory that we will have in the resurrection will depend on how much of Christ we have gained during this process of the salvation of our souls. "There is one glory of the sun, and another glory of the moon, and another glory of the stars: for one star differeth from another star in glory. So also is the resurrection of the dead" (I Corinthians 15:41-42, KJV).

Paul writes in Philippians 3:7-9, "But whatever were gains to me I now consider loss for the sake of Christ. What is more, I consider everything a loss because of the surpassing worth of knowing Christ Jesus my Lord, for whose sake I have lost all things. I consider them garbage, that I may gain Christ and be found in him, not having a righteousness of my own that comes from the law, but that which is through faith in Christ—the righteousness that comes from God on the basis of faith." We, like Paul, must count everything of the flesh that we used to boast in as loss, for the excellency of knowing Christ Jesus as Lord.

Paul continues in verses 10 and 11, "My goal is to know Him and the power of His resurrection and the fellowship of His sufferings, being conformed to His death, assuming that I will somehow reach the resurrection from among the dead" (HCSB). The goal of our Christian life must be to know Him, and the power of His resurrection, and the fellowship of His sufferings.

We also, like Paul, should strive to attain to the resurrection from the dead. This word translated as "resurrection" in verse 11 is used only one time in Scripture. Its literal translation is the "out-resurrection." Apparently, based on Paul's desire to attain unto it, it must be the best resurrection. This probably refers to the resurrection in Revelation 20, the first resurrection, where those that are resurrected rule and reign with Christ for 1,000 years.

We must count everything as loss that would interfere with our knowing Christ. Christ must be the preeminent focus of our life. We must not become caught up in the cares of this life and the love of money.

It is never too late! Right now, we can repent and turn again to the Lord, looking away to Him, beholding and reflecting Him. We can redeem the time; we can buy it back by being filled with the Spirit. "See then that ye walk circumspectly, not as fools, but as wise, Redeeming the time, because the days are evil. Wherefore be ye not unwise, but understanding what the will of the Lord is. And be not drunk with wine, wherein is excess; but be filled with the Spirit; Speaking to yourselves in psalms and hymns and spiritual songs, singing and making melody in your heart to the Lord; Giving thanks always for all things unto God and the Father in the name of our Lord Jesus Christ; Submitting yourselves one to another in the fear of God" (Ephesians 5:15-21, KJV).

After we have been saved by being born again, we begin the process of our soul being saved. This process of the salvation of the soul continues from the time of Christ, as the Spirit, coming to indwell our spirit until our physical body dies or the Lord returns. Then this phase of the salvation process, the salvation of our soul, ends. The next phase of our salvation begins when the dead are raised at the last trump. Then we begin a new, virtually instant, process of salvation, the salvation of our bodies. In a moment, in the twinkling of an eye, we will be changed.

Paul writes in I Corinthians 15:50-53. "Now I say this, brethren, that flesh and blood cannot inherit the kingdom of God; nor does the perishable inherit the imperishable. Behold, I tell you a mystery; we will not all sleep, but we will all be changed, in a moment, in the twinkling of an eye, at the last trumpet; for the trumpet will sound, and the dead will be raised imperishable, and we will be changed. For this perishable must put on the imperishable, and this mortal must put on immortality."

As you can see, there is a lot more to salvation than most people realize. My prayer is that we will each continue steadfast in the faith and endure to the end until we all reach maturity in Christ, that we might be found in Him, not having a righteousness of our own, but the righteousness of faith. Hebrews 10:24-25 instructs us, "Let us consider one another to provoke unto love and good works: Not forsaking the assembling of ourselves together, as the manner of some is; but exhorting one another: and so much the more, as ye see the day approaching" (KJV). We must continue to assemble together that we might encourage one another, and even more as the day of the Lord draws near.

Paul writes in Philippians 3:12-15, "Not that I have already obtained it or have already become perfect, but I press on so that I may lay hold of that for which also I was laid hold of by Christ Jesus. Brethren, I do not regard myself as having laid hold of it yet; but one thing I do: forgetting what lies behind and reaching forward to what lies ahead, I press on toward the goal for the prize of the upward call of God in Christ Jesus. Let us therefore, as many as are perfect (mature), have this attitude."

Chapter 5 Discussion Questions: Understanding Salvation

1. What does the Greek word sozo mean?
2. What is meant by temporal salvation?
3. What is meant by the salvation of the spirit?
4. What part of our being is made alive when we are born again?
5. What process begins once a believer is born again?
6. How long does this process last?
7. What things does Christ as the indwelling Spirit work to accomplish in the believer?
8. How does He accomplish these things?
9. What is the goal or the end result of our faith?
10. How is the believer freed from the power and dominion of sin?
11. How does the Lord use trials and times of suffering in the life of the believer?

12. How will believers differ in glory in the resurrection?
13. What happens during the salvation of our bodies?
14. What did Paul do to attain unto the out-resurrection of the dead?

REMEMBER THE SABBATH

Remember the Sabbath day, to keep it holy.
(Exodus 20:8)

The LORD said to Moses in Exodus 31:13-17, "Tell the Israelites: You must observe My Sabbaths, for it is a sign between Me and you throughout your generations, so that you will know that I am Yahweh who sets you apart. Observe the Sabbath, for it is holy to you. Whoever profanes it must be put to death. If anyone does work on it, that person must be cut off from his people.

"Work may be done for six days, but on the seventh day there must be a Sabbath of complete rest, dedicated to the LORD. Anyone who does work on the Sabbath day must be put to death. The Israelites must observe the Sabbath, celebrating it throughout their generations as a perpetual covenant. It is a sign forever between Me and the Israelites, for in six days the LORD made the heavens and the earth, but on the seventh day He rested and was refreshed" (HCSB).

The Sabbath is a sign between the Lord and His people. It was given as a sign so that the Lord's people would know that He is the Lord who sanctifies them. They are not to do any work on the Sabbath. To work on the Sabbath is to defile it. Anyone who works on the Sabbath will be cut off from his people. The Sabbath must be observed as a day of complete rest. The Lord made the heavens and the earth in six days, and on the seventh day He rested and was refreshed. The Lord's people are likewise expected to rest on the seventh day.

Man is allotted by God six days in which to do his work. Then on the seventh day he must observe a day of complete rest. By observing a day of complete rest, he is honoring that day as a remembrance that it is the Lord who sanctifies them. When they sanctify the Sabbath as a day of complete rest, they are reminded that the Lord sanctifies them. They observe the day in remembrance of the Lord and His sanctifying work of setting them apart as holy unto Himself.

The Lord declares in Isaiah 58:13, "If you keep your feet from breaking the Sabbath and from doing as you please on my holy day, if you call the Sabbath a delight and the LORD's holy day honorable, and if you honor it by not going your own way and not doing as you please or speaking idle words, then you will find your joy in the LORD" (NIV).

Remembering the Sabbath and honoring it by not going our own way and doing as we please should be a delight to the Lord's people. If we regard the Sabbath as delightful, then we will find our joy in the Lord.

Jesus told the Pharisees, "The Sabbath was made for man, and not man for the Sabbath. So the Son of Man is Lord even of the Sabbath" (Mark 2:27-28).

The Sabbath was intended to be a blessing for God's people. It was to be a delight to them. It was to be refreshing as it turned their thoughts to remember that the Lord is the one that sanctifies them. They were to be honored to set the Sabbath apart as holy because God had set them apart as holy.

God sent Moses to deliver the children of Israel out of bondage and oppression in Egypt and bring them into the promised land of Canaan. The promised land was to be a Sabbath to them where they would find rest from oppression and the attacks of their enemies, where God would protect them, provide for them, and fight their battles.

However, the children of Israel rebelled and hardened their hearts. Their hearts turned away from God in unbelief and longed to return to Egypt. Therefore, God became angry with them and swore that they would not enter into His rest.

Hebrews 3:7-4:3 admonishes us, "Today, if you hear his voice, do not harden your hearts as you did in the rebellion, during the time of testing in the wilderness, where your ancestors tested and tried me, though for forty years they saw what I did. That is why I was angry with that generation; I said, 'Their hearts are always going astray, and they have not known my ways.' So I declared an oath in my anger, 'They shall never enter my rest.'

"See to it, brothers and sisters, that none of you has a sinful, unbelieving heart that turns away from the living God. But encourage one another daily, as long as it is called 'Today,' so that none of you may be hardened by sin's deceitfulness. We have come to share in Christ, if indeed we hold our original conviction firmly to the very end. As has just been said: 'Today, if you hear his voice, do not harden your hearts as you did in the rebellion.'

"Who were they who heard and rebelled? Were they not all those Moses led out of Egypt? And with whom was he angry for forty years? Was it not with those who sinned, whose bodies perished in the wilderness?

"And to whom did he swear they would never enter into his rest, except those who were disobedient? So we see that they could not enter because of unbelief.

"Therefore we must be wary that, while the promise of entering his rest remains open, none of you may seem to have come short of it. For we had good news proclaimed to us just as they did. But the message they heard did them no good, since they did not join in with those who heard it in faith. For we who have believed enter that rest" (NIV).

The children of Israel rebelled in the wilderness and failed to enter into the rest that God had prepared for them. They failed to enter into God's rest because of a heart of unbelief. A hardened, sinful heart does not believe God's promise. It does not believe that God loves us and wants the best for us. A sinful, unbelieving heart does not trust that God's provision for us is adequate to satisfy all of our needs. It is not confident that God's provision is enough.

The good news is that God has prepared a rest for us today. He has prepared a rest for anyone who will believe His promise that He made to Abraham. God promised Abraham thousands of years ago that all the nations of the earth would be blessed through Abraham's seed. That seed has arrived. That seed is Christ.

Christ, through perfect obedience to God, lived a sinless life and died a sacrificial death, shedding His blood to atone for our sins, that we might have peace with God. Through the power of the resurrection, the way has been opened for us to enter, by the blood of Jesus, into God's presence and into His rest.

Hebrews 4:9-11 says, "There remains a Sabbath rest for the people of God. For the one who has entered His rest has himself also rested from his works, as God did from His. Therefore let us be diligent to enter that rest, so that no one will fall, through following the same example of disobedience."

In order to enter into God's rest, we must believe that God raised Jesus from the dead, demonstrating His total satisfaction and approval of Christ's sinless life and sacrificial death as sufficient to atone for our sins. By the resurrection from the dead, God made this Jesus both Lord and Christ (Acts 2:32-36). He has given all authority onto Him (Matthew 28:18). It is through faith in Jesus that we have peace with God.

By faith in Jesus, we are placed by God into Christ; and Christ, in the person of the Holy Spirit, is placed into us (I Corinthians 1:30, Romans 8:9-11). By this Spirit of the glorified Christ being deposited into us by God, we are born again. Upon being born again, the Holy Spirit dwells within our spirit to teach us all that is ours in Christ. Christ, as the indwelling Holy Spirit, enables us to live holy lives pleasing to the Lord. He equips us and strengthens us to do everything that God requires from us. We can, through the empowering and leading of the Holy Spirit, do all things through Christ who strengthens us (Philippians 4:13).

Ezekiel 44:18 says that God's servants are not to sweat in His presence. God does not want us to serve Him out of our natural effort. He only wants us to serve Him trusting in the power of the Spirit working within us to enable us to obey Him. We must realize that in ourselves we have no ability to please God. Apart from Christ, we can do nothing (John 15:5). We must abide in Christ and trust Him to provide us with everything we need by His Spirit that dwells within us.

Our faith in Jesus is demonstrated by our willingness to accept the completed work of Christ as sufficient for our justification. Our faith in Jesus is also demonstrated by our willingness to cease from our own works. A believing heart does not attempt to perform any works of the law in order to enhance our justification before God. A believer's confidence in coming to God is in Jesus Christ alone, and His blood shed for our justification. Faith in Jesus is enough. That faith will produce works that are done fully trusting in Christ and His rich provision for our every need.

Paul writes in Galatians 3:1-18, "You foolish Galatians! Who has hypnotized you, before whose eyes Jesus Christ was vividly portrayed as crucified? I only want to learn this from you: Did you receive the Spirit by the works of the law or by hearing with faith? Are you so foolish? After beginning with the Spirit, are you now going to be made complete by the flesh? Did you suffer so much for nothing—if in fact it was for nothing? So then, does God supply you with the Spirit and work miracles among you by the works of the law or by hearing with faith?

"Just as Abraham believed God, and it was credited to him for righteousness, then understand that those who have faith are Abraham's sons. Now the Scripture saw in advance that God would justify the Gentiles by faith and told the good news ahead of time to Abraham, saying, 'All the nations will be blessed through you.' So those who have faith are blessed with Abraham, who had faith.

"For all who rely on the works of the law are under a curse, because it is written: Everyone who does not continue doing everything written in the book of the law is cursed. Now it is clear that no one is justified before God by the law, because the righteous will live by faith. But the law is not based on faith; instead, the one who does these things will live by them. Christ has redeemed us from the curse of the law by becoming a curse for us, because it is written: 'Everyone who is hung on a tree is cursed.' The purpose was that the blessing of Abraham would come to the Gentiles by Christ Jesus, so that we could receive the promised Spirit through faith.

"Brothers, I'm using a human illustration. No one sets aside or makes additions to even a human covenant that has been ratified. Now the promises were spoken to Abraham and to his seed. He does not say 'and to seeds', as though referring to many, but referring to one, and to your seed, who is Christ. And I say this: The law, which came 430 years later, does not revoke a covenant that was previously ratified by God and cancel the promise. For if the inheritance is from the law, it is no longer from the promise; but God granted it to Abraham through the promise" (HCSB).

Galatians 3:21-29 asks, "Is the law then against the promises of God? God forbid: for if there had been a law given which could have given life, verily righteousness should have been by the law. But the Scripture hath concluded all under sin, that the promise by faith of Jesus Christ might be given to them that believe.

"But before faith came, we were kept under the law, shut up unto the faith which should afterwards be revealed. Wherefore the law was our schoolmaster to bring us unto Christ, that we might be justified by faith. But after that faith is come, we are no longer under a schoolmaster."

The purpose of the law was to bring us to Christ, that believing in Christ, we might be justified by faith. But now, having been justified by faith, we are no longer under the law. Colossians 2:16-17 warns us, "Therefore do not let anyone judge you by what you eat or drink, or with regard to a religious festival, a New Moon celebration or a Sabbath day. These are a shadow of the things that were to come; the reality, however, is found in Christ" (NIV).

The reality is Christ! The feasts, the new moon, the Sabbath days, these are only shadows of that which was to come. They are shadows of Christ. They are shadows of the real thing. That real thing that cast these shadows is Christ Jesus our Lord! Why would we continue to cling to the shadows when we have the reality, the Christ that cast the shadows?

Jesus is the real rest. Jesus is the real Sabbath. It is Jesus that we need to remember and set apart as holy. It is only as we remember and honor Him, who sanctified us by His blood, and rest from our own works, that we can have real rest.

Paul reminds us in Galatians 2:16 "that a man is not justified by the works of the Law but through faith in Christ Jesus, even we have believed in Christ Jesus, so that we may be justified by faith in Christ and not by the works of the Law; since by the works of the Law no flesh will be justified."

As believers we must be continually reminded that Christ is our Sabbath. We must be reminded that His sinless life and His sacrificial death are sufficient to satisfy God's righteous and holy requirements for our atonement and justification.

Paul admonishes us again in Galatians 5:4, "You who are trying to be justified by the law are alienated from Christ; you have fallen from grace" (HCSB). We must learn to rest completely in Christ's finished work of redemption, and not continue to strive to be justified by the works of the law, because by the works of the law no one will be justified. "For whoever keeps the whole law and yet stumbles at just one point is guilty of breaking all of it" (James 2:10, NIV).

What does it mean for a believer to "Remember the Sabbath?" It means to cease from our own works and totally rest in the completed redemption work of Christ. It means to honor Christ by believing in Him and setting Him apart as holy, believing that His blood is sufficient for our justification.

Being set free from the dominion of sin and empowered by the indwelling Holy Spirit to live a holy life in full obedience to God is the essence of the Sabbath rest. It is here, abiding in Christ, our Sabbath, that we truly have rest because He is our peace.

When we come to know Jesus as the indwelling Spirit that is always with us to teach us, to comfort us, and to guide, equip, and strengthen us in all that God would have us do, then we truly have entered into His rest and have ceased from our own works. It is here that we truly find joy unspeakable, full of glory, "Remembering the Sabbath and keeping it holy."

When we walk by the Spirit, we are keeping the Sabbath! When we walk by the Spirit, every day is an observance of the Sabbath and an enjoyment of the Sabbath rest.

Chapter 6 Discussion Questions: Remember the Sabbath

1. Why were the Israelites required to keep the Sabbath?
2. How were the children of Israel to honor the Sabbath?
3. What was intended by God to be a Sabbath for Israel so they could find rest from their enemies?

4. Who was unable to enter that rest, and why were they unable to enter into God's rest?
5. How do we enter into God's rest?
6. How is our faith in Jesus demonstrated?
7. What was the purpose of the Law?
8. What things are only shadows of Christ?
9. Who is our real Sabbath?
10. When are we really keeping the Sabbath?

THE BLESSEDNESS OF GIVING

Jesus said, "A new commandment I give to you, that you love one another, even as I have loved you, that you also love one another. By this all men will know that you are My disciples, if you have love for one another" (John 13:34).

"We know love by this, that He laid down His life for us; and we ought to lay down our lives for the brethren. But whoever has the world's goods, and sees his brother in need and closes his heart against him, how does the love of God abide in him? Little children, let us not love with word or with tongue, but in deed and truth" (I John 3:16-18).

Under the law of the first covenant, God commanded the tithe, or the tenth, as a means of providing for the Levites as they did the work of the service in the Lord's tabernacle, as well as the foreign residents, the fatherless, the widows and the priests. However, the law of the first covenant was fulfilled in Christ as He took away the first covenant to establish the second.

"The former regulation is set aside because it was weak and useless (for the law made nothing perfect), and a better hope is introduced, by which we draw near to God" (Hebrews 7:19, NIV). Hebrews 8:6 tells us, "Jesus has now obtained a superior ministry, and to that degree He is the mediator of a better covenant, which has been legally enacted on better promises" (HCSB).

"He then says, 'See I have come to do your will.' He takes away the first to establish the second. By this will, we have been sanctified through the offering of the body of Jesus Christ once and for all" (Hebrews 10:9, HCSB). This offering of the body of Jesus Christ, once and for all, has made the offerings and the sacrifices of the old covenant obsolete. They are no longer needed, as Jesus has fully satisfied God's righteous requirements for our atonement and forgiveness.

"Christ hath redeemed us from the curse of the law, being made a curse for us: for it is written, Cursed is every one that hangeth on a tree: That the blessing of Abraham might come on the Gentiles through Jesus Christ; that we might receive the promise of the Spirit through faith" (Galatians 3:14-15, KJV).

Galatians 5:1 and 6 reminds us, "It was for freedom that Christ set us free; therefore keep standing firm and do not be subject again to a yoke of slavery (the law). For in Christ Jesus neither circumcision nor uncircumcision means anything, but faith working through love." Neither tithing nor not tithing means anything, but faith working through love. Under the new covenant, we don't give because the law requires us to. We give because the love of God that has been poured out in our hearts, and we therefore love one another and give joyfully and generously in obedience to the leading of the indwelling Holy Spirit.

Tithing was a part of the law of the first covenant which has been taken away to establish the second covenant. There is no longer any need for all the offerings and sacrifices of the first covenant because we have been sanctified through the offering of the body of Jesus Christ once and for all.

We find no admonition in the new covenant for believers to present any of the offerings or sacrifices of the old covenant. However, we find several admonitions to provide for those of our own household, to give to the poor, and especially to the brothers, and to those that labor to serve the Lord.

In Matthew 6:1-4, Jesus offers advice on how to give. He says, "Beware of practicing your righteousness before men to be noticed by them; otherwise you have no reward with your Father who is in heaven. So when you give to the poor, do not sound a trumpet before you, as the hypocrites do in the synagogues and in the streets, so that they may be honored by men. Truly I say to you, they have their reward in full. But when you give to the poor, do not let your left hand know what your right hand is doing, so that your giving will be in secret; and your Father who sees what is done in secret will reward you."

Paul writes in Galatians 2:9-10, "Recognizing the grace that had been given to me, James and Cephas and John, who were reputed to be pillars, gave to me and Barnabas the right hand of fellowship, so that we might go to the Gentiles and they to the circumcised. They only asked us to remember the poor—the very thing I also was eager to do."

Paul, in his farewell address to the elders from the church in Ephesus in Acts 20:34-35, says, "You yourselves know that these hands ministered to my own needs and to the men who were with me. In everything I showed you that by working hard in this manner you must help the weak and remember the words of the Lord Jesus, that He Himself said, 'It is more blessed to give than to receive.'"

We should not be dependent on others. Rather, we should work diligently to provide for the needs of our own household and to have an excess to be able to help provide for others (I Thessalonians 4:9-12; 2 Thessalonians 3:11-12; Ephesians 4:28).

Notice in the New Testament the continual encouragement to give to the poor, without any encouragement, from the day of Pentecost on, to tithe to the church. However, tithing is encouraged and even required by some churches to enable them to have huge elaborate buildings. We don't need huge, elaborate buildings to meet in. Simple functional structures would be quite sufficient for the Lord's work. The early church often met in homes. These smaller sized gatherings allowed the opportunity for every member of the body to be intimately acquainted with the needs of every other member of the body.

One of the great things about giving directly to the poor is that it requires us to look to the Lord for direction about who to give to and how much and when and how to give. When someone tithes to their church, it is easy. It does not require any relationship with the Lord. Basically, they are just paying someone else to seek the Lord and decide where and how their money should be distributed.

When someone desiring to keep the law tithes to their church, they may feel that they have done their legally required religious duty. They may feel they have paid their share, and they might expect that the poor will be taken care of and that they themselves will receive a well-prepared and well-delivered sermon, as well as a well-maintained facility. Tithing can give a false sense of righteousness without any real relationship with the Lord.

However, all are greatly benefited when each looks in faith to the Lord. Some will be greatly blessed as they look to the Lord for the provision of their needs. Others will be greatly blessed when they look to the Lord for where, when and how much to give. Living by faith and giving by faith are very important aspects of growing in Christ.

Jesus tells the rich young man in Matthew 19:21, "If you want to be perfect, go, sell your belongings and give to the poor, and you will have treasure in heaven. Then come, follow me" (HCSB). Give to the poor and you will have treasure in heaven.

In 2 Corinthians 9:6-8, Paul says, "Remember this: the person who sows sparingly will also reap sparingly, and the person who sows generously will also reap generously. Each person should do as he has decided in his heart – not out of regret or out of necessity, for God loves a cheerful giver. And God is able to make every grace overflow to you, so that in every way, always having everything you need, you may excel in every good work" (HCSB).

Proverbs 11:24 says, "One person gives freely, yet gains more; another withholds what is right, only to become poor" (HCSB). Proverbs 19:17 says, "Kindness to the poor is a loan to the Lord, and He will give a reward to the lender" (HCSB).

Ecclesiastes 11:1-2 says, "Send your bread on the surface of the water, for after many days you may find it. Give a portion to seven or even to eight, for you don't know what disaster may happen on earth" (HCSB). James 1:27 says, "Pure and undefiled religion before our God and Father is this: to look after orphans and widows in their distress and to keep oneself unstained by the world" (HCSB).

Paul writes in Galatians 6:6-10, "The one who is taught the word is to share all good things with the one who teaches him. Do not be deceived, God is not mocked; for whatever a man sows, this he will also reap. For the one who sows to his own flesh will from the flesh reap corruption, but the one who sows to the Spirit will from the Spirit reap eternal life. Let us not lose heart in doing good, for in due time we will reap if we do not grow weary. So then, while we have opportunity, let us do good to all people, and especially to those who are of the household of the faith."

Under the law of the old covenant, everyone was required to give a tenth; that was the Lord's share. Under the new covenant, the Holy Spirit has poured the love of God abroad in our hearts (Romans 5:5) and has given us a love for the brothers whereby we would gladly lay down our life for the brothers. With born-again believers, a tenth should be the minimum in our giving, with a desire that we would be able to give as much and as freely as the Lord would provide. However, this tenth should not be observed as a legal requirement.

Paul reminds us in I Corinthians 6:19-20, "You are not your own. You were bought at a price" (NIV). We are the Lord's; and everything we have is the Lord's. Jesus says in Matthew 10:8, "Freely you have received, freely give" (NIV). Acts 4:32 says the believers in the early church in Jerusalem "were of one heart and soul, and no one said that any of his possessions was his own" (HCSB). If the Lord reveals to us someone in need, especially a believer, and we have the means to help them, we should give generously as the Lord directs.

Jesus tells us in Luke 6:30-35, "Give to everyone who asks of you, and whoever takes away what is yours, do not demand it back. Treat others the same way you want them to treat you. If you love those who love you, what credit is that to you? For even sinners love those who love them. If you do good to those who do good to you, what credit is that to you? For even sinners do the same. If you lend to those from whom you expect to receive, what credit is that to you? Even sinners lend to sinners in order to receive back the same amount. But love your enemies, and do good, and lend, expecting nothing in return; and your reward will be great, and you will be sons of the Most High; for He Himself is kind to ungrateful and evil men."

Jesus continues in verse 38, "Give, and it will be given to you. They will pour into your lap a good measure—pressed down, shaken together, and running over. For by your standard of measure it will be measured to you in return."

"We know love by this, that He laid down His life for us; and we ought to lay down our lives for the brethren. But whoever has the world's goods, and sees his brother in need and closes his heart against him, how does the love of God abide in him? Little children, let us not love with word or with tongue, but in deed and truth" (I John 3:16-18).

The faithful overseer, deacon, or shepherd should be provided for by those they serve. Whether you give to your church for their support or give to them directly, your giving, how much, to whom, and when, should be totally by faith, in complete and humble obedience to the Lord's leading. Whether you give to your church or give directly to the Lord's servants, to the poor, to widows and orphans, to the brothers and sisters in the faith, or to support those of your own relatives, do it joyfully and generously, that God would be glorified, and not legally as one under the law attempting to be justified according to the works of the flesh.

May we be victorious Christians in our giving, the Lord blessing us with a cheerful heart as we give generously in obedience to His leading.

Chapter 7 Discussion Questions: The Blessedness of Giving

1. What was the new commandment that Jesus gave His disciples?
2. How do we know love?
3. What is the tithe?
4. Why is the tithe not required under the new covenant?
5. In the first covenant the Law was written of tablets of stone, where were they written in the new covenant?
6. Is there a need for tithing under the new covenant?
7. Under the new covenant, how are we admonished to give?
8. What is one of the great benefits of giving directly to the poor?
9. As believers, how much should we give?
10. Who should we give to?
11. What does it mean to live by faith and to give by faith?
12. Why should we be joyful, generous givers?

SECTION 2 – THE CHURCH – A SPIRITUAL HOUSE

ONE NEW MAN - THE CHURCH

Paul wrote to the Gentile believers in Ephesians 2:11-22 saying, "Therefore remember that formerly you, the Gentiles in the flesh, who are called 'Uncircumcision' by the so-called 'Circumcision,' which is performed in the flesh by human hands— remember that you were at that time separate from Christ, excluded from the commonwealth of Israel, and strangers to the covenants of promise, having no hope and without God in the world. But now in Christ Jesus you who formerly were far off have been brought near by the blood of Christ.

"For He Himself is our peace, who made both groups into one and broke down the barrier of the dividing wall, by abolishing in His flesh the enmity, which is the Law of commandments contained in ordinances, so that in Himself He might make the two into one new man, thus establishing peace, and might reconcile them both in one body to God through the cross, by it having put to death the enmity. AND HE CAME AND PREACHED PEACE TO YOU WHO WERE FAR AWAY, AND PEACE TO THOSE WHO WERE NEAR; for through Him we both have our access in one Spirit to the Father.

"So then you are no longer strangers and aliens, but you are fellow citizens with the saints, and are of God's household, having been built on the foundation of the apostles and prophets, Christ Jesus Himself being the corner stone, in whom the whole building, being fitted together, is growing into a holy temple in the Lord, in whom you also are being built together into a dwelling of God in the Spirit."

How many times have we heard that Christ died on the cross to pay for our sins, and to reconcile us to God? Yet here Paul is not referring to Christ's death on the cross from the perspective of our individual reconciliation to God. Paul is revealing here a great mystery. This mystery is that Christ's death on the cross was to reconcile two groups into one by tearing down the dividing wall of hostility. Who are these two groups?

Paul refers here to the "circumcised" and the "uncircumcised." He refers to those that were of the citizenship of Israel and those "excluded" from the citizenship of Israel. Paul is speaking here of two groups, the Jews and the Gentiles.

Christ created in Himself one new man from the two, from the Jews and the Gentiles. He did this that He might reconcile both to God in one body through the cross and put the hostility between the two groups to death by it.

So now the Gentiles are no longer foreigners and strangers, but fellow citizens with the saints and members of God's household. Now the Jews and Gentiles are built together on the same foundation, the foundation of the apostles and the prophets, with Christ Jesus Himself as the cornerstone.

This one new man is the church, the body of Christ. It is composed of all the believers, the people of faith, the children of promise, from the time of Adam until the

Lord's return. They all have been made members of this one body, this one new man, the church. This church has become the demonstration of the manifold wisdom of God to the rulers and authorities in heavenly places.

Paul continues to explain this in Ephesians 3:1-12, "For this reason I, Paul, the prisoner of Christ Jesus for the sake of you Gentiles— if indeed you have heard of the stewardship of God's grace which was given to me for you; that by revelation there was made known to me the mystery, as I wrote before in brief. By referring to this, when you read you can understand my insight into the mystery of Christ, which in other generations was not made known to the sons of men, as it has now been revealed to His holy apostles and prophets in the Spirit; to be specific, that the Gentiles are fellow heirs and fellow members of the body, and fellow partakers of the promise in Christ Jesus through the gospel, of which I was made a minister, according to the gift of God's grace which was given to me according to the working of His power.

"To me, the very least of all saints, this grace was given, to preach to the Gentiles the unfathomable riches of Christ, and to bring to light what is the administration of the mystery which for ages has been hidden in God who created all things; so that the manifold wisdom of God might now be made known through the church to the rulers and the authorities in the heavenly places. This was in accordance with the eternal purpose which He carried out in Christ Jesus our Lord, in whom we have boldness and confident access through faith in Him."

At the very heart of this mystery is that the Gentiles are coheirs, members of the same body, and partners of the promise in Christ Jesus through the gospel. The Gentiles are co-heirs with whom? They are co-heirs with the Jews, with the children of Israel, with the sons of Abraham. The believing Gentiles are members of the same body as the believing Jews. These Gentiles are partners of the same promise in Christ Jesus through obedience to the gospel.

This is something that every believer, Jew and Gentile alike, needs to be keenly aware of. Jesus accomplished God's eternal purpose on the cross by making the two groups into one new man in Himself. God's eternal purpose is to have one body, prepared as a bride, without spot or wrinkle. It is for this bride that Christ is returning. God's eternal purpose is that of a loving father longing to have a spotless bride to present to His son. This is the ultimate expression of God's love.

Why is it so important for us to see and understand this mystery of the two being made one new man in Christ? This is critical because throughout the ages there has been an animosity, a hostility between the Jew and the Gentile. This is clearly manifested even in our day in the constant trouble in the Middle East. The world cannot have peace because of this hostility.

In the church, we can only have peace when we clearly understand that, by the blood of Christ, this hostility has been removed, and the dividing wall has been torn down. Whenever any believer is truly born again and the love of God is shed abroad in their heart, whether Jew or Gentile, this wall is torn down, and there is peace. By this, there is a deep realization of our oneness in Christ, which produces a genuine love for all the brothers, regardless of natural birth, regardless of whether they are Jews or Gentiles.

In Christ, we are all one. It is in this oneness that we are both reconciled to God. We are reconciled to God in one body through the cross. It is through the cross that this hostility has been put to death. When we died with Christ, the hostility between believers according to our flesh died also. It is by the death of this hostility that we are made one in Christ, resulting in peace.

When we see the necessity of this oneness between the Jewish believers and the Gentile believers for the accomplishment of God's eternal purpose, it is very troubling to hear so-called believers teach that there is a difference between the Jews and the Gentiles. Some teach that there are different rewards, different manifestations of the kingdom, and so on. Some teach that some Scriptures apply only to the Jews and that some Scriptures apply only to the Gentiles. Some have even divided the body based on whether the believer is by natural birth a Jew or a Gentile.

Perhaps they teach these destructive, divisive things because, being devoid of the Spirit, they can only see things according to the flesh. Having no understanding of spiritual things, they cannot understand the mysteries hidden for ages of God's eternal purpose in Christ. They see things according to physical descent and not according to faith.

Paul tells us clearly in Romans 2:28, "For a person is not a Jew who is one outwardly, and true circumcision is not something visible in the flesh. On the contrary, a person is a Jew who is one inwardly, and circumcision is of the heart—by the Spirit, not the letter. That man's praise is not from men but from God."

Paul continues to make this point in Galatians 3:6-9, "Just as Abraham believed God, and it was credited to him for righteousness, then understand that those who have faith are Abraham's sons. Now the Scripture saw in advance that God would justify the Gentiles by faith and told the good news ahead of time to Abraham, saying, 'All the nations will be blessed through you.' So those who have faith are blessed with Abraham, who had faith." Paul continues in verse 14, "The purpose was that the blessing of Abraham would come to the Gentiles by Christ Jesus, so that we could receive the promised Spirit through faith."

Paul continues this thought in verses 16-19, "Now the promises were spoken to Abraham and to his seed. He does not say 'and to seeds,' as though referring to many, but referring to one, and to your seed, who is Christ. And I say this: The law, which came 430 years later, does not revoke a covenant that was previously ratified by God and cancel the promise. For if the inheritance is from the law, it is no longer from the promise; but God granted it to Abraham through the promise. Why then was the law given? It was added because of transgressions until the Seed to whom the promise was made would come."

Paul concludes his thoughts in verses 22-29, "But the Scripture has imprisoned everything under sin's power, so that the promise by faith in Jesus Christ might be given to those who believe. Before this faith came, we were confined under the law, imprisoned until the coming faith was revealed. The law, then, was our guardian until Christ, so that we could be justified by faith. But since that faith has come, we are no longer under a guardian, for you are all sons of God through faith in Christ Jesus. For as many of you as have been baptized into Christ have put on Christ like a garment. There is no Jew or Greek, slave or free, male or female; for you are all one in Christ Jesus. And if you belong to Christ, then you are Abraham's seed, heirs according to the promise."

In Romans 9:6-8 Paul says, "But it is not as though the word of God has failed. For not all who are descended from Israel are Israel. Neither are they all children because they are Abraham's descendants. On the contrary, your offspring will be traced through Isaac. That is, it is not the children by physical descent who are God's children, but the children of the promise are considered to be the offspring."

In Romans 11:17-32 Paul continues, "Now if some of the branches were broken off, and you, though a wild olive branch, were grafted in among them and have come to share in the rich root of the cultivated olive tree, do not brag that you are better than those branches. But if you do brag—you do not sustain the root, but the root sustains you. Then you will say, 'Branches were broken off so that I might be grafted in.' True enough; they were broken off by unbelief, but you stand by faith. Do not be arrogant, but be afraid. For if God did not spare the natural branches, He will not spare you either.

"Therefore, consider God's kindness and severity: severity toward those who have fallen but God's kindness toward you—if you remain in His kindness. Otherwise you too will be cut off. And even they, if they do not remain in unbelief, will be grafted in, because God has the power to graft them in again. For if you were cut off from your native wild olive and against nature were grafted into a cultivated olive tree, how much more will these—the natural branches—be grafted into their own olive tree?

"So that you will not be conceited, brothers, I do not want you to be unaware of this mystery: A partial hardening has come to Israel until the full number of the Gentiles has come in. And in this way all Israel will be saved, as it is written: The Liberator will come from Zion; He will turn away godlessness from Jacob. And this will be My covenant with them when I take away their sins.

"Regarding the gospel, they are enemies for your advantage, but regarding election, they are loved because of the patriarchs, since God's gracious gifts and calling are irrevocable. As you once disobeyed God, but now have received mercy through their disobedience, so they too have now disobeyed, resulting in mercy to you, so that they also now may receive mercy. For God has imprisoned all in disobedience, so that He may have mercy on all."

From these passages, it is clear that physical descent is meaningless. It is the spiritual reality that counts. It is not the children by physical descent who are God's children. Only the children of the promise are considered to be the offspring. Those who have faith, whether they are Jews or Gentiles, are truly Abraham's sons. It is only through disobedience and unbelief that any are cut off from the promise.

It is also important to understand that time is irrelevant as concerns God through Christ making of the two one new man. Christ made the two, the Jewish believers and the Gentile believers, into one body. It is irrelevant whether these believers were alive before Christ's birth or after Christ's death. They are all children of promise, people of faith in God. They had a faith, like Abraham, that believing God, it was credited to them as righteousness.

This one body that Christ made from the two, includes all believers of all ages or eras. They are all a part of the church, the body of Christ.

Hebrews 11 recounts all the heroes of faith and the things that they endured for the testimony of the Lord. It mentions Abel, Enoch, Noah, Abraham, Isaac, Jacob, Joseph, Moses, Rahab, Samuel, and so on. All people of faith. Some Jews, some Gentiles, some from before there were Jews and Gentiles. All people of faith, children of promise.

Verses 39-40 say, "And all these, having gained approval through their faith, did not receive what was promised, because God had provided something better for us, so that apart from us they would not be made perfect (complete)." They could not be made perfect; they could not be completed without us. They were a part of something that was not yet completed, and could not be completed without us. They could not receive what was promised until what they were a part of was completed.

Chapter 12 of Hebrews continues with verses 1-2 saying, "Therefore, since we have so great a cloud of witnesses surrounding us, let us also lay aside every encumbrance and the sin which so easily entangles us, and let us run with endurance the race that is set before us, fixing our eyes on Jesus, the author and perfecter of faith." The cloud of witnesses referred to here are those mentioned in chapter 11 that are waiting for us to arrive at the unity of faith and the maturity of the fulness of the stature of Christ that they might receive what was promised.

These witnesses, these heroes of faith, need us to finish the race. They need us to be perfected so that they might be perfected with us. They are cheering us on to run the race, to lay aside every obstacle and the sin that so easily entangles us. They are cheering for us to be continually looking away to Jesus, the author and finisher of our faith.

They, together with us, are the church, the body of Christ. Together, we will be the bride that our Lord Jesus Christ is returning for, a bride without spot or wrinkle. A bride fully prepared for her husband.

The thought of being built into the same habitation, the same body, with Peter and Paul, and with Abraham, Moses, and Rahab, the thought of being one in Christ with all the saints is absolutely incredible. We, together, are one new man in Christ. Time can place no constraints on our God. God, however, uses time to put constraints on man. When a person dies, that person's time to repent and to receive mercy from God runs out.

God has imprisoned all in disobedience that He may have mercy on all. That mercy, and the resulting sonship that is available to all, is only available by faith, by faith in Christ who is Abraham's seed. If you belong to Christ, you are Abraham's seed, heirs according to the promise. In the end, all Israel will be saved, that is all that are of faith, all that are children of the promise, whether Jews or Gentiles. Only the unbelievers, whether Jews or Gentiles will perish and miss out on the blessings of the promise.

The writer of Hebrews says in Hebrews 10:29-31: "How much worse punishment do you think one will deserve who has trampled on the Son of God, regarded as profane the blood of the covenant by which he was sanctified, and insulted the Spirit of grace? For we know the One who has said, Vengeance belongs to Me, I will repay, and again, The Lord will judge His people. It is a terrifying thing to fall into the hands of the living God!" (HCSB).

It is not a small thing to build up what God in Christ has torn down or to divide in two what God has made one. It is not a small thing to be found fighting against God and His eternal purpose. Colossians 3:11 assures us that "In Christ there is not Greek and Jew, circumcision and uncircumcision, barbarian, Scythian, slave and free; but Christ is all and in all" (HCSB).

John tells us in Revelation 21:1-4, "Then I saw a new heaven and a new earth, for the first heaven and the first earth had passed away, and the sea no longer existed. I also saw the Holy City, New Jerusalem, coming down out of heaven from God, prepared like a bride adorned for her husband. Then I heard a loud voice from the throne: Look! God's dwelling is with humanity, and He will live with them. They will be His people, and God Himself will be with them and be their God. He will wipe away every tear from their eyes. Death will no longer exist; grief, crying, and pain will exist no longer, because the previous things have passed away" (HCSB).

Again in verse nine John goes on to describe this holy city, the New Jerusalem saying, "Then one of the seven angels, who had held the seven bowls filled with the seven last plagues, came and spoke with me: 'Come, I will show you the bride, the wife of the Lamb.' He then carried me away in the Spirit to a great and high mountain and showed me the holy city, Jerusalem, coming down out of heaven from God, arrayed with God's glory.

"Her radiance was like a very precious stone, like a jasper stone, bright as crystal. The city had a massive high wall, with 12 gates. Twelve angels were at the gates; the names of the 12 tribes of Israel's sons were inscribed on the gates. There were three gates on the east, three gates on the north, three gates on the south, and three gates on the west. The city wall had 12 foundations, and the 12 names of the Lamb's 12 apostles were on the foundations" (HCSB).

Here at the very end of the Bible, at the end of the last book, we see the fulfillment of God's eternal purpose. Here we see the holy city, New Jerusalem, coming down out of heaven from God, prepared as a bride adorned for her husband. Here we see the bride spoken of in Ephesians chapter 5, without spot or wrinkle, holy and blameless, the wife of the Lamb.

Notice that in this description of the bride, the New Jerusalem, the names of the 12 tribes of Israel are inscribed on the gates. Notice also that the names of the Lamb's 12 apostles are on the foundations. Even in the final consummation of God's eternal purpose, the Jews and the Gentiles, from all the ages of time, the children of promise, the church, are forever together sharing the same destiny. They, together, are the bride of Christ.

Revelation 22:3-5 reveals: "The throne of God and of the Lamb will be in it, and His bond-servants will serve Him; they will see His face, and His name will be on their foreheads. And there will no longer be any night; and they will not have need of the light of a lamp nor of the light of the sun, because the Lord God will illumine them; and they will reign forever and ever."

Let us heed the words of Paul in Ephesians 4:1-6: "Therefore I, the prisoner for the Lord, implore you to walk in a manner worthy of the calling with which you have been called, with all humility and gentleness, with patience, showing tolerance for one another in love, being diligent to preserve the unity of the Spirit in the bond of peace. There is one body and one Spirit, just as also you were called in one hope at your calling; one Lord, one faith, one baptism, one God and Father of all who is over all and through all and in all."

Let us walk in a manner worthy of our glorious Lord, redeeming the time, making the most of every opportunity to prove our love for one another and for our God.

Chapter 8 Discussion Questions: One New Man – The Church

1. Who are the circumcised and who are the uncircumcised?
2. What was the purpose of Christ's death on the cross, beyond paying for our sins.

3. What two groups did Christ reconcile to God in one body?
4. What is this mystery that has been hidden for ages?
5. Who are the Gentiles co-heirs with?
6. How is the manifold wisdom of God demonstrated?
7. How did Jesus accomplish God's eternal purpose?
8. Why is it so important for us to see and understand this mystery?
9. How has the hostility between the Jews and the Gentiles been put to death?
10. According to Galatians 3, who are Abraham's sons?
11. According to Romans 9, who are God's children?
12. What are the heroes of faith in Hebrews 11 waiting for?
13. What is the cloud of witnesses surrounding us in Hebrews 12 composed of?
14. Why do those in Hebrews 11 need those in Hebrews 12?

THE HEAD OF THE CHURCH

The church is an organism, a living body composed of the many people who have been born again by believing in, submitting to, and confessing the Lordship of Jesus, the Christ. The word "church" means the assembly of the called-out ones. This refers to the gathering together of those who have been born of the Spirit and called out of the world unto God.

These born-again, Spirit-filled Christians are all members of the body of Christ. This is one body with many members. This one body of Christ is expressed in every city, town or village where these born-again believers assemble together, holding Christ alone as their head. The Scriptures refer to the church in Corinth, the church in Ephesus, the church in Laodicea, the churches of Judea, the churches of Asia, and the church that is in their house.

These called out ones look to Jesus to guide and direct them both individually, in their daily lives, and corporately, as they assemble together as the church, His living body. These Christians tolerate no person usurping the headship that is reserved only for their Lord, Jesus the Christ.

Colossians 2:18-19 warns us of those who would seek to defraud us of our prize in Christ being fleshly minded "and not holding fast the head, from which the entire body, being supplied and held together by the joints and ligaments, grows with a growth which is from God." It is essential, if the church is to be healthy and grow, that it hold fast to Christ as its head, diligently rejecting any and all who would seek to usurp Christ's place as the one and only head of the church.

Throughout His time on earth, Jesus continually taught His disciples. One lesson He stressed to them repeatedly was that of His unique place as head of the assembly, the church. He stressed that no one should exalt themselves over any other person in the church.

The day after Jesus and His disciples had come down from the Mount of Transfiguration, an argument started among the disciples as to who would be the greatest. Jesus, knowing the thoughts of their hearts, took a little child to Himself, and told His disciples: "For whoever is least among you – this one is great" (Luke 9:46-48, HCSB).

Then they left that place and made their way through Galilee and came to Capernaum. In the house at Capernaum, in response to another argument that had arisen among His disciples along the way concerning which of them was the greatest. Jesus said to them: "If anyone wants to be first, he must be last of all, and servant of all" (Mark 9:33-35, HCSB).

Again, while on their way up to Jerusalem, Jesus took His disciples aside privately and said to them; "You know that the rulers of the Gentiles dominate them, and the men of high position exercise power over them. It must not be like that among you" (Matthew 20:25-26, HCSB).

And again, immediately after the "last supper," just before Jesus was arrested and crucified, He again admonished His disciples, sharing with them the thing that was most heavy upon His heart. Jesus said to them: "The kings of the Gentiles dominate them, and those who have authority over them are called 'Benefactors.' But it must not be like that among you. On the contrary, whoever is greatest among you must become like the youngest, and whoever leads, like the one serving" (Luke 22:25-26, HCSB).

Not only did Jesus stress this matter repeatedly to His disciples, He also confronted the religious leaders of His day concerning their arrogant ungodly behavior. Speaking to the crowds and to His disciples about the religious leaders in Matthew 23:2-13 Jesus said: "The scribes and the Pharisees have seated themselves in the chair of Moses; therefore all that they tell you, do and observe, but do not do according to their deeds; for they say things and do not do them. They tie up heavy burdens and lay them on men's shoulders, but they themselves are unwilling to move them with so much as a finger. But they do all their deeds to be noticed by men; for they broaden their phylacteries and lengthen the tassels of their garments.

"They love the place of honor at banquets and the chief seats in the synagogues, and respectful greetings in the market places, and being called Rabbi by men. But do not be called Rabbi; for One is your Teacher, and you are all brothers. Do not call anyone on earth your father; for One is your Father, He who is in heaven.

"Do not be called leaders; for One is your Leader, that is, Christ. But the greatest among you shall be your servant. Whoever exalts himself shall be humbled; and whoever humbles himself shall be exalted. But woe to you, scribes and Pharisees, hypocrites, because you shut off the kingdom of heaven from people; for you do not enter in yourselves, nor do you allow those who are entering to go in."

This is why these Christians, assembling together as the true church, tolerate no person usurping the headship that is reserved only for the Lord, Jesus the Christ. Jesus said in Matthew 18:20: "Where two or three are gathered together in my name, I am there among them." Christ leads during the assembly, and the believers follow. This body, thus, is living and vibrant, every member ministering one to another, freely giving and receiving from one another, as their Lord, Jesus, has freely given to them.

Jesus gave apostles, prophets, evangelists, shepherds, and teachers as gifts to the church for the training, the equipping of the saints. The saints then are to do the work of the ministry, the work of building up the church by being obedient to the leading of the Holy Spirit as He directs each one. Christ, as the indwelling Holy Spirit, tells each one what to say and when to say it. The saints are trained to prophesy, to lift up Jesus, speaking forth Christ, both in the meetings and in their daily lives.

These trainers train the saints to know the indwelling Holy Spirit and to hear His voice. The saints are trained to listen to the Spirit's speaking and to be diligent to obey. This training is to continue until we all arrive at the unity of the faith and maturity in Christ. The saints are to be trained to know and use the gifts of the Holy Spirit to serve one another and to build up the church, the body of Christ.

By this ministering of every member, this prophesying, this speaking the truth to one another in love, the body is built up, edified, made strong in the strength of the Lord by that which every joint supplies (1 Corinthians 14:26-33). Ephesians 4:15-16 says, "Speaking the truth in love, we are to grow up in all aspects into Him who is the head, even Christ, from whom the whole body, being fitted and held together by what every joint supplies, according to the proper working of each individual part, causes the growth of the body for the building up of itself in love." This is the church as seen in the Bible.

Paul explains in I Corinthians 3 how the church, the body of Christ, is built up by the work of these gifted members of the body building on the one foundation that has been laid, that is Christ Himself as the foundation stone. Paul plants and Apollos waters, but God makes the seed to grow. "The planter and the waterer are nothing compared to Him who gives life to the seed. The planter and the waterer are alike insignificant, though each shall be rewarded according to his particular work" (I Corinthians 3:7-8, Phillips). Although Paul and Apollos are apostles, neither is anything, but God in Christ is everything. The one who plants is nothing and the one who waters is nothing. But God, who gives life to the seed, is everything.

According to Paul in Ephesians 5:21, all believers are to submit to one another out of reverence for Christ. In humility, we are to esteem each other as better than ourselves (Philippians 2:4). John the Baptist said in John 3:30 that Christ must increase, and that he, John, must decrease. This needs to be the attitude of every believer. We must never desire to be anything. Rather, our desire must be that Christ would be everything. We must desire that Christ be the preeminent one, that He would be the one and only head of the church.

"My people did not listen to My voice, And Israel did not obey Me. So I gave them over to the stubbornness of their heart, to walk in their own devices. Oh that My people would listen to Me, that Israel would walk in My ways! I would quickly subdue their enemies and turn My hand against their adversaries. Those who hate the LORD would pretend obedience to Him" (Psalm 81:11-15).

When we usurp the place of Christ as head of the church, we are pretending obedience to Him. In reality, we are refusing to listen to His voice and are walking in our own devices, in the stubbornness of our evil hearts. When we do this, we weaken the church and lay it open to attack from the enemy. If we would repent and obey the Lord, He would subdue the enemy and heal the divisions within the church.

Whenever we find ourselves desiring to be something, a huge red flag should go up to warn us that we are not walking by the Spirit, but by the flesh. We must immediately repent, humble ourselves, and turn our hearts afresh to the Lord Jesus Christ, the head of the church.

Here in the church, while holding Christ as head, we each have every opportunity and responsibility to minister to, and receive from, one another, as Christ directs. We do this by esteeming each other as better than ourselves, that through every joint of supply, the body might build itself up in love.

When we steadfastly hold Christ as head, He will build His church. This is what Christ is longing for. He desires a body, built up and mature, as a bride prepared for His return, looking to Him alone as its head.

Chapter 9 Discussion Questions: The Head of the Church

1. What is the meaning of the term "church" as used in Scripture?
2. Who is the head of this church?
3. What lesson did Jesus stress repeatedly to His disciples?
4. What are some of the things that Jesus accused the religious leaders of His day of doing
5. When two or more believers are gathered together, who leads the assembly?
6. Who are the trainers in the church?
7. What are they training the saints to do?
8. How are we to grow up in all aspects into Him who is the head?
9. Who did Paul say was nothing?
10. What should the attitude of every believer be?
11. What should our reaction be if we ever find ourselves desiring to be something in the church?

BUILDING THE CHURCH

I have visited an untold number of churches of widely varying denominations. Often during these visits, I would find myself in the middle of very thoughtful and concerned discussions on how they can build their church. Often the discussions focus on increasing membership, increasing attendance, increasing revenues, increasing staff, replacing staff, changing the music, changing the décor, increasing programs, increasing facilities, building new facilities, utilizing social media, and so on. There are virtually unlimited ways that are proposed to address the problem of how to build a church. How can we know what is the best approach to use?

I believe, as with any other problem, we must begin by gaining a thorough understanding of the problem that we are trying to address. What exactly are we hoping to accomplish? What do we mean by building a church?

To many people, the idea of building a church means to build up and strengthen the organization in which their church exists. This organization is composed of bylaws, a constitution, a governing board, and the staff they direct and the facilities and programs that they operate and maintain. So, it is only natural that they are concerned with all of the items mentioned above that are often the focus of their discussions on how to build their church.

However, in this brief study, I am not going to focus on how to build up a modern church organization, but rather on how to build up the church as set forth in the Scriptures. This church in the New Testament is not an organization. It is an organism, a living body. It is the body of the resurrected Christ.

This living body is composed of a multitude of people. These people are believers in Jesus Christ. These believers have been born again. They have been born of the Holy Spirit. These believers, upon being born again, have become living members of this living body of Jesus Christ, the church.

Our consideration in this study will be focused on how to build this church, the living body of the resurrected Christ. For guidance in this study, we will rely on the leading of the Holy Spirit and the teaching of the Holy Scriptures. So, as the Spirit directs, we will review various passages of Scripture and consider how they address the question of how to build the church.

Jesus said in John 3:14, "As Moses lifted up the serpent in the wilderness, even so must the Son of Man be lifted up." Again, Jesus tells us in John 12:32, "And I, if I am lifted up from the earth, will draw all men to Myself." Finally, in Matthew 16:18, Jesus promises, "I will build My church."

Wow, this sounds so simple. Jesus promises that He will build His church. He promises that if He is lifted up, He will draw all people to Himself. So, what is required of us?

If Jesus will draw all people to Himself and He will build His church, what else is needed? What are we expected to do for the church to be built up?

It is necessary, just as Moses lifted up the snake in the wilderness, so the Son of Man, Jesus, must be lifted up. This is our job. This is our portion of the work of building up the church. We are expected to lift up Jesus. He will then draw all men to Himself, and He will build His church.

So, how are we expected to accomplish our part of this task of building the church? To gain an understanding of God's expectation of us as born-again believers, let us search the Scriptures for instruction.

In the book of Numbers 21:4-9, we read the account of the children of Israel murmuring and complaining, speaking against God and Moses. In response to this the Lord God sent poisonous snakes among the people, and the snakes bit them so that many Israelites died.

Then Moses interceded for the people, praying to God for deliverance from the snakes. God told Moses to make a bronze snake and mount it on a pole. God told him that whenever anyone that was bitten looks at the snake, they would recover.

This is the same message that we have for the world today. The poisonous venom of the serpent, the devil, has infected the entire human race with the deadly, rebellious sin nature. The only way that anyone can be delivered from the dominance and control of this rebellious sin nature is to look by faith to the Son of Man, Jesus.

When anyone believes and looks to Jesus for deliverance from the power of sin that leads to death, they will be saved. They will be delivered, set free from bondage, from slavery to sin. They will be set free to serve God in newness of life, in the newness of the new life that they receive in Jesus.

So, we can lift up Jesus by sharing with people that are lost and dying about the deliverance from the power of sin and of death that is freely available to anyone, simply by looking in faith to Jesus. No matter who they are or what they have done, if they will turn the eyes of their heart to Jesus, He will set them free and give them a new life, free from the power of sin and of death (Romans 6:1-14).

Once a person is born again by looking to Jesus and receiving a new life in the Spirit, they become members of the body of Christ, the church. As members of His body, they embark on a new journey. This is a life-long journey of growing in faith and being conformed to the image of Jesus Christ the Lord. This conformation, this transformation, is accomplished by the Holy Spirit that comes to dwell within every genuine believer. This indwelling Spirit transforms us into the image of Christ as we behold and reflect the Lord. This work of transformation is the Spirit's doing (2 Corinthians 3:15-18).

The only requirement of the believer is that he continues, just as he began this salvation process, looking away to Jesus. We must continue to look away to Jesus, because He is the author and the finisher of our faith. We began our walk of faith by looking to Jesus; we can only complete this walk, arriving at maturity in Christ, by continuing to look to Jesus.

To build the church, we need to lift up Jesus, that people might be saved through faith, looking to Him. Also, to build the church, we need to lift up Jesus, that people might grow to maturity in Christ looking to Him. So, whether to be born again by the Spirit or to be transformed by the Spirit, we need to look to Jesus.

We have seen how we can lift up Jesus that unbelievers might be saved by looking to Him. But, how do we lift up Jesus so that believers might be transformed and brought to maturity in Christ? I think we can also find the answer to this in the Scriptures.

Paul writes in Colossians 1:28, "We proclaim Him (Jesus), warning and teaching everyone with all wisdom, so that we may present everyone mature in Christ" (HCSB). What does Paul do to help believers grow unto maturity in Christ? It is very simple. He proclaims Christ! He lifts up Jesus and encourages the believers to continue to look to Jesus, walking by the Spirit.

In I Corinthians 14:26-33, Paul writes about what happens when believers gather together for worship. He says each one has a psalm, a teaching, a revelation, let everything be done for the building up of the church. He says two or three prophets should speak, and the others sitting by should evaluate. He says if something is revealed to someone sitting there listening to the prophets, the prophet should be silent and should let the person that received the revelation speak.

Paul continues saying, "You can all prophecy, one by one, so that everyone may learn and that everyone may be encouraged" (HCSB). Whenever an apostle, a prophet, or an ordinary believer that has received a revelation, speaks being led by the Holy Spirit, everyone can learn, and everyone can be encouraged. When anyone speaks being led by the Holy Spirit, Jesus is exalted. He is lifted up, and the believers grow in their faith.

Whenever any believer speaks in obedience to the leading of the Holy Spirit, Jesus is lifted up. As the believers then look to Jesus, they are fed, they are encouraged, and they are being transformed by the Holy Spirit and are being brought on toward maturity in Christ. The church is being built up.

In Ephesians 4:11-13, Paul tells us that Jesus "gave some to be apostles, some prophets, some evangelists, some pastors and teachers, for the training of the saints in the work of ministry, to build up the body of Christ, until we all reach unity in the faith and in the knowledge of God's Son, growing into a mature man with a stature measured by Christ's fullness" (HCSB).

Notice that the apostles, prophets, evangelists, pastors, and teachers were given for one purpose, for the training of the saints. They were given to train the saints to do the work of the ministry. The work of the ministry is to be done by the saints. The work of the ministry that the saints are supposed to be doing is the building up of the body of Christ.

Also, notice how long these apostles, prophets, evangelists, pastors, and teachers are supposed to continue training the saints. They are to continue their work of training the saints until we all reach unity in the faith and grow into a mature man measured by the stature of Christ's fullness. Have we arrived? If not, then the training work of the apostles, prophets, evangelists, pastors, and teachers must not be complete, and certainly the work of the ministry of the saints, to build up the body of Christ, is not complete.

The apostles, prophets, evangelists, pastors, and teachers are to train the saints to know the leading of the indwelling Holy Spirit, so the saints can learn to hear the Spirit speaking and to faithfully obey the Lord's leading them by the Holy Spirit. Then the saints, by the leading of the Spirit and the guidance and oversight of their trainers grow in faith and maturity and become effective at lifting up Jesus, by speaking what the Spirit gives them to speak, when and how He tells them to speak.

Paul explains in verses 15-16 the practical application of this process where he says, "Speaking the truth in love, we are to grow up in all aspects into Him who is the head, even Christ, from whom the whole body, being fitted and held together by what every joint supplies, according to the proper working of each individual part, causes the growth of the body for the building up of itself in love."

From Christ, the whole body grows, fitted and knit together by every supporting ligament, by the proper working of each individual part speaking the truth in love, growing in every way into Christ who is the head. Jesus said in John 14:6, "I am the way, and the truth and the life." When we speak the truth in love, we are speaking forth Christ, and Jesus is lifted up.

When the saints speak forth Christ in obedience to the leading of the Holy Spirit, everyone is able to learn, and everyone is encouraged. Paul writes in I Corinthians 14:23-25, "Therefore if the whole church assembles together and . . . if all prophesy (speak forth Christ), and an unbeliever or an ungifted man enters, he is convicted by all, he is called to account by all; the secrets of his heart are disclosed; and so he will fall on his face and worship God, declaring that God is certainly among you."

When Jesus is lifted up, the hearts of unbelievers will be touched and brought to account, and the hearts of believers will be touched, taught, and encouraged. When Jesus is lifted up, He will draw all people to Himself. He will build His church.

The most exciting thing is that every born-again believer has the opportunity and the ability by obeying the leading of the indwelling Holy Spirit to lift Jesus up, whether in the assembly of the church or in the course of their daily lives.

The genuine church, the church that Jesus is building, provides this opportunity for every born-again believer to prophesy, to speak forth Christ, to lift Jesus up. It also trains the believers to faithfully take advantage of this opportunity in the assembly of the church, where everyone can prophesy, one by one, that all might learn and that all might be encouraged, that the church might be built up.

Chapter 10 Discussion Questions: Building the Church

1. How do you build up a modern church organization?
2. How do you build a church as set forth in Scripture?
3. Why did Moses lift up the serpent in the wilderness?
4. Why must Jesus be lifted up?
5. Who will build the church as set forth in Scripture?
6. How can people be saved from their rebellious sinful nature?
7. How can we grow in faith and be conformed to the image of Jesus?
8. What did Paul do to bring everyone to maturity in Christ?
9. What is the purpose of the apostles, prophets, evangelists, pastors, and teachers?
10. Who trains the saints to speak forth the truth in love?
11. What does it mean to speak the truth in love?
12. What happens when all the saints speak forth Christ in obedience to the leading of the Holy Spirit?

BEING BUILT UP TOGETHER

"Now you are Christ's body, and individually members of it." (I Corinthians 12:27). For this reason, we need to accept one another and be willing to be built up together with one another. We must not allow minor disagreements to divide and separate us from one another.

Some of the most encouraging, most edifying fellowship I have enjoyed has been with brothers that had a totally different understanding, a totally different perspective on important issues of the faith. We need to be tolerant. We need to listen. We need to be willing to calmly discuss issues without becoming emotionally attached to what we have been taught and have embraced for years.

We need to be able to gather together with brothers of widely different backgrounds and discuss our beliefs and go to the Scriptures and examine rationally the basis for each perspective. We need to be able to do this, not to prove that we are right, but together, to reach a deeper, more scriptural understanding of God and of His ways. We each need to be humble enough to be taught by the Spirit and to be willing to give up any teaching of man that we may have adopted when we find it to be contrary to Scripture.

We need to trust God that His Spirit within us is able, by the love of God that has been poured abroad in our hearts, to empower us to love brothers with whom we do not agree on every issue. We need to be willing to fellowship together, disagreeing at times on various issues, and yet embracing each other as brothers in Christ, as members of the one body, being built up together as a spiritual habitation of God in the Spirit.

I Peter 2:1-5 says, "Therefore, putting aside all malice and all deceit and hypocrisy and envy and all slander, like newborn babies, long for the pure milk of the word, so that by it you may grow in respect to salvation, if you have tasted the kindness of the Lord. And coming to Him as to a living stone which has been rejected by men, but is choice and precious in the sight of God, you also, as living stones, are being built up as a spiritual house for a holy priesthood, to offer up spiritual sacrifices acceptable to God through Jesus Christ."

We are living stones being built up together into a spiritual house for a holy priesthood. If we are going to be built up together, we need to esteem the other as better than ourselves, and not to think more highly of ourselves than we ought.

Paul encourages us in Philippians 2:1-8, "Therefore if there is any encouragement in Christ, if there is any consolation of love, if there is any fellowship of the Spirit, if any affection and compassion, make my joy complete by being of the same mind, maintaining the same love, united in spirit, intent on one purpose.

"Do nothing from selfishness or empty conceit, but with humility of mind regard one another as more important than yourselves; do not merely look out for your own personal interests, but also for the interests of others. Have this attitude in yourselves which was also in Christ Jesus, who, although He existed in the form of God, did not regard equality with God a thing to be grasped, but emptied Himself, taking the form of a bond-servant, and being made in the likeness of men. Being found in appearance as a man, He humbled Himself by becoming obedient to the point of death, even death on a cross."

In the New Testament, we never see more than one church in any city. We see the church in Jerusalem, the church in Ephesus, and the church in Colossae. We see references to multiple churches in regions or countries: the churches in Galatia, the churches in Judea, and the churches in Asia. Some of these churches met in homes. But even in Jerusalem, where more than 8,000 believers were reported as being saved in Acts chapters 2 and 4, there is no record of more than one church in that city.

Instead, the believers met together daily, in the temple and from house to house, breaking bread together. The believers met with those that happened to be living near them. There is no record in Scripture of believers seeking out a church where they were more comfortable, or where the people all agreed on every issue.

No, God placed them in the church, in the body, as it pleased Him. The believers were focused on Christ and His grace that had been poured out on them. God has not changed. He still places believers in the body as it pleases Him.

I John 4:20-21 says, "If someone says, 'I love God,' and hates his brother, he is a liar; for the one who does not love his brother whom he has seen, cannot love God whom he has not seen. And this commandment we have from Him, that the one who loves God should love his brother also."

In I Corinthians 12:4-10, Paul identifies several spiritual gifts. "Now there are different gifts, but the same Spirit. There are different ministries, but the same Lord. And there are different activities, but the same God activates each gift in each person. A demonstration of the Spirit is given to each person to produce what is beneficial" (HCSB).

He continues in I Corinthians 12:11-27, "All these are the work of one and the same Spirit, and he distributes them to each one, just as he determines. Just as a body, though one, has many parts, but all its many parts form one body, so it is with Christ. For we were all baptized by one Spirit so as to form one body—whether Jews or Gentiles, slave or free—and we were all given the one Spirit to drink. Even so the body is not made up of one part but of many.

"Now if the foot should say, 'Because I am not a hand, I do not belong to the body,' it would not for that reason stop being part of the body. And if the ear should say, 'Because I am not an eye, I do not belong to the body,' it would not for that reason stop being part of the body. If the whole body were an eye, where would the sense of hearing be? If the whole body were an ear, where would the sense of smell be? But in fact God has placed the parts in the body, every one of them, just as he wanted them to be. If they were all one part, where would the body be? As it is, there are many parts, but one body.

"The eye cannot say to the hand, 'I don't need you!' And the head cannot say to the feet, 'I don't need you!' On the contrary, those parts of the body that seem to be weaker are indispensable, and the parts that we think are less honorable we treat with special honor. And the parts that are unpresentable are treated with special modesty, while our presentable parts need no special treatment. But God has put the body together, giving greater honor to the parts that lacked it, so that there should be no division in the body, but that its parts should have equal concern for each other. If one part suffers, every part suffers with it; if one part is honored, every part rejoices with it. Now you are the body of Christ, and each one of you is a part of it" (NIV).

We need to understand that each member of the body has been given certain gifts by God and placed in the body as it has pleased Him. There are many parts, yet one body. "The eye cannot say to the hand, 'I don't need you!' Or again, the head can't say to the feet, 'I don't need you!'"

Unfortunately, the body of Christ has been divided into many parts. Some of these parts insist that only those that are exactly like them can be a part of their church. What we end up with is the church of the eyes on one street, the church of the ears on another street, the church of the hands on another street, and the church of the heads on yet another street.

We have failed to realize that God has placed each member in the body, living in close proximity to each other, for the effectual building up of the body of Christ. We have chosen where we worship, what church we join, based on our preferences and our comfort level, rather than on where God has placed us. We have put a priority on our comfort and our acceptance by man, receiving honor from one another, instead of receiving honor from God. We meet with the church of our choice and have gladly joined the division of greatest comfort.

God sovereignly places believers in neighborhoods, in towns, where there are other believers. His expectation is that these believers would bow to His sovereign arrangement and fellowship with the believers that He has placed near them. If we are not able to fellowship with the believers that God has placed nearest to us, perhaps it reveals something about whether we are really loving the brothers. Perhaps we are only willing to love the brothers that make us comfortable.

Jesus said in Matthew 16:24, "If anyone wishes to come after Me, he must deny himself, and take up his cross and follow Me. For whoever wishes to save his life will lose it; but whoever loses his life for My sake will find it." Jesus tells us in Mark 10:29-30, "Truly I say to you, there is no one who has left house or brothers or sisters or mother or father or children or farms, for My sake and for the gospel's sake, but that he will receive a hundred times as much now in the present age, houses and brothers and sisters and mothers and children and farms, along with persecutions; and in the age to come, eternal life."

If we are willing to trust the Lord and follow Him, giving up our comfort, our preferences, He promises to place us in His family as it pleases Him. We need to decide. What do we care more about? Do we care more about our comfort and our preferences, or do we care more about being built up together in the body of Christ, right where God has placed us?

Chapter 11 Discussion Questions: Being Built up Together

1. What does I Peter 2:1-5 say that we are being built into?
2. What does this passage refer to each of us as?
3. How does Paul in Philippians 2 say believers should regard one another?

4. Over 8,000 were recorded as becoming Christians in Jerusalem in Acts 2-4, how many churches did they have?

5. How often did these believers gather together?

6. Where did they meet?

7. What did they do during these meetings?

8. Do all the believers that were baptized by one Spirit to form one body have the same gifts and background?

9. Who has put all of these diverse believers into one body?

10. What does it mean that God has placed each of us into the body as it has pleased Him?

11. Why do many believers travel from the neighborhood they live in to fellowship with a church in a different area?

12. What do we need to do if we are to be built up into a spiritual house where God has placed us in the body?

SPIRITUAL GIFTS

Paul writes in I Corinthians 14:1-5, "Pursue love and desire spiritual gifts, and above all that you may prophesy. For the person who speaks in another language is not speaking to men but to God, since no one understands him; however, he speaks mysteries in the Spirit. But the person who prophesies speaks to people for edification, encouragement, and consolation. The person who speaks in another language builds himself up, but he who prophesies builds up the church. I wish all of you spoke in other languages, but even more that you prophesied. The person who prophesies is greater than the person who speaks in languages, unless he interprets so that the church may be built up" (HCSB).

The word "prophesy" here means to tell forth, or to speak forth. Specifically, in this context it means to speak forth something for Christ, something that the indwelling Holy Spirit has given you and instructed you to speak to the church. It may be only five words, but if it is five words given to you by the Holy Spirit it will be used by the Spirit to build up the church.

In this brief passage, there are several important points that Paul is trying to make. First, he is stressing the supreme importance of prophesying. He says, "Pursue love and desire spiritual gifts, and above all that you may prophesy." The reason he says, "Above all that you may prophesy," is so that the church would be built up. "He who prophesies builds up the church." For Paul, the ultimate goal of the Christian life is that the church, the body of Christ, would be built up, that it would be "without spot or wrinkle or any such thing, but holy and blameless," "like a bride adorned for her husband" (Ephesians 5:27; Revelation 21:2, HCSB).

Paul continues in I Corinthians 14:26-33, "What then is the conclusion, brothers? Whenever you come together, each one has a psalm, a teaching, a revelation, another language, or an interpretation. All things must be done for edification. If any person speaks in another language, there should be only two, or at the most three, each in turn, and someone must interpret. But if there is no interpreter, that person should keep silent in the church and speak to himself and to God.

"Two or three prophets should speak, and the others should evaluate. But if something has been revealed to another person sitting there, the first prophet should be silent. For you can all prophesy one by one, so that everyone may learn and everyone may be encouraged. And the prophets' spirits are under the control of the prophets, since God is not a God of disorder but of peace" (HCSB).

Notice that Paul says, "You can all prophesy one by one." For a believer to prophesy does not require some special gift. You don't have to be a prophet in order to prophesy. You simply need to be sensitive to the speaking of the Holy Spirit as He gives you something to speak and be diligent to obey and boldly speak forth what you were told to speak.

In addition to prophesying that the church might be built up, Paul also encourages the saints to "pursue love and desire spiritual gifts." This is consistent with his over-riding desire that the church be built up. Brothers loving one another is a basic foundational requirement for the building up of the church. Without the brothers loving one another, the church cannot be built up. It is for this reason that Jesus gives the church a new commandment in John 13:34. "A new commandment I give to you, that you love one another, even as I have loved you, that you also love one another."

In keeping with his desire for building up the church, in addition to his encouragement to the believers that they may prophesy and pursue love, he also instructs them to desire spiritual gifts. His reason for this is obviously the same as his reason to encourage them to prophesy and to pursue love, that the church be built up.

What are these "spiritual gifts" that Paul encourages the saints to desire? In I Corinthians 12:4-10 Paul identi-fies several spiritual gifts. "Now there are different gifts, but the same Spirit. There are different ministries, but the same Lord. And there are different activities, but the same God activates each gift in each person. A demonstration of the Spirit is given to each person to produce what is beneficial: to one is given a message of wisdom through the Spirit, to another, a message of knowledge by the same Spirit, to another, faith by the same Spirit, to another, gifts of healing by the one Spirit, to another, the performing of miracles, to another, prophecy, to another, distinguishing between spirits, to another, different kinds of languages, to another, interpretation of languages" (HCSB).

In Romans 12:6-8, Paul mentions other gifts. "According to the grace given to us, we have different gifts: If prophecy, use it according to the standard of one's faith; if service, in service; if teaching, in teaching; if exhorting, in exhortation; giving, with generosity; leading, with diligence; showing mercy, with cheerfulness" (HCSB). All the spiritual gifts Paul lists have obvious uses for the building up of the church, by teaching, by exhorting, by encouraging, by increasing faith, by caring, helping and loving one another.

In I Corinthians 12:27-31, Paul goes so far as to rank some of these gifts in order of importance in the church. "Now you are the body of Christ, and individual members of it. And God has placed these in the church: first apostles, second prophets, third teachers, next miracles, then gifts of healing, helping, managing, various kinds of languages." He also makes it clear in this passage that none of the gifts is possessed by every believer. "Are all apostles? Are all prophets? Are all teachers? Do all do miracles? Do all have gifts of healing? Do all speak in other languages? Do all interpret?" (HCSB). The obvious answer is "No, not all are apostles, not all are prophets." There is not one gift that is possessed by all or required to be possessed by all.

Notice also that Paul does not ask here if all can prophesy, but rather he asks, "Are all prophets?" Clearly all are not prophets, however, as Paul stated in I Corinthians 14:31, "You can all prophesy one by one." Again, to prophesy does not require that you have the gift of being a prophet. All born-again believers can prophesy, speaking in obedience to the leading of the indwelling Holy Spirit.

Paul concludes saying, "But desire the greater gifts." Yes, we should desire the greater gifts, that of apostles, prophets, teachers, miracles, healing, helping, and managing. Notice that the last gift mentioned, and by implication, the one that we should desire least is that of various kinds of languages. The reason for this is clear. "The person who speaks in another language builds himself up, but he who prophesies builds up the church." It is much more desirable that our focus be on building up the church, rather than on building up ourselves.

If our purpose is to build up the church, the body of Christ, where are these gifts in the church today? As we look about, we notice that most of these gifts seem strangely absent. We must ask ourselves the reason why. What happened to the gifts that we are told that we should desire?

There is a teaching that has been propagated within some churches based on an interpretation of I Corinthians 13:8-12. "Love never fails; but if there are gifts of prophecy, they will be done away; if there are tongues, they will cease; if there is knowledge, it will be done away. For we know in part and we prophesy in part; but when the perfect comes, the partial will be done away."

The teaching states that "when the perfect comes, the partial will be done away" refers to the completion of the Scriptures. So, they say, when the New Testament was completed, the perfect had come, and there was no longer a need for these gifts of the Spirit. This, however, is not consistent with the context of the passage of Scripture from which this is taken. If we examine the context, we see that an entirely different interpretation is indicated.

The passage continues, "For now we see in a mirror dimly, but then face to face; now I know in part, but then I will know fully just as I also have been fully known." Here Paul is saying that "now we see in a mirror dimly" referring to the time he was writing this letter. "Then" refers to "when the perfect comes." Then he will see clearly, face to face. He says, "now I know in part, but then," when the perfect comes, he will know fully as he also has been fully known.

Can any one of us honestly say, "I see face to face," or "I know fully just as I also have been fully known?" If we say these things, then we are saying that we see more clearly than Paul did, and that we know more fully than Paul did. As for me, there is no way I could even begin to think, much less say, these things.

It becomes clear that "when the perfect comes" refers to Christ's return. It is only then that we will see face to face or know as we are fully known. It is interesting that there is another passage that has been misunderstood in a very similar way.

Paul writes in Ephesians 4:11-13, "And He gave some as apostles, and some as prophets, and some as evangelists, and some as pastors and teachers, for the equipping of the saints for the work of service, to the building up of the body of Christ; until we all attain to the unity of the faith, and of the knowledge of the Son of God, to a mature man, to the measure of the stature which belongs to the fullness of Christ." In conjunction with the misinterpretation that we just examined of I Corinthians 13 and the cessation of the gifts of the Spirit, this passage in Ephesians has been interpreted saying that the apostles and prophets are no more.

The natural conclusion of the teaching that the gifts of the Spirit have ceased and that which is perfect is the completion of the Scriptures, is that people serving as pastors, teachers, evangelists are not the result of the Spirit's gifting, but of the training received in Bible colleges and seminaries. The teaching that results is that there are no apostles or prophets today. They were only needed for the establishment and foundation of the church, but now that we have the completed Scriptures, they are no longer needed.

However, if we examine the context of this passage of Ephesians, we will notice that it tells us clearly how long these gifts of apostles, prophets, evangelists, pastors, and teachers will continue. It says, "Until we all attain to the unity of the faith, and of the knowledge of the Son of God, to a mature man, to the measure of the stature which belongs to the fullness of Christ." Again, I would simply ask, have we attained? Have we all attained to the unity of the faith? What about all the divisions in Christianity? Have we matured and grown into the stature which belongs to the fullness of Christ? I believe the answer is clearly, "NO!"

It is clear that the gifts of the Spirit have not ceased. They are desperately needed today for the building up of the church. These false teachings have produced a heart of unbelief in some churches, especially as regards the operation of the gifts of the Spirit. Instead of trusting the Holy Spirit's gifting of the members of the body of Christ for the building up of the church, we have come to trust the teachings of man and the training of man by the institutions of man.

John 5:44 says, "How can you believe? While accepting glory from one another, you don't seek the glory that comes from the only God." We must be those that believe the Scriptures, accepting what they say, not trying to twist them to fit our doctrines and desires to exalt ourselves and receive glory from one another. We need to seek the glory that comes from God.

This level of unbelief reminds me of Matthew 13:58, which says, "And He (Jesus) did not do many miracles there because of their unbelief." Also, Mark 6:5, which says, "So He was not able to do any miracles there, except that He laid His hands on a few sick people and healed them. And He was amazed at their unbelief" (HCSB). Perhaps the absence of the gifts of the Spirit in some churches is due to the unbelief that has resulted from these false teachings. We need to believe the Scriptures and we need to believe that gifts of the Spirit have been given to each believer to produce that which is beneficial for the building up of the body of Christ.

Let us not be like the servant that received the one talent and, because of fear and unbelief, went out and hid his talent, burying it in the ground. When his master returned, he called him a wicked, slothful servant, and had him cast into outer darkness where there will be weeping and gnashing of teeth.

Rather, let us be like those that received talents and immediately went out and put their talents to work. When their master returned, he said to them, "Well done, good and faithful servant. You have been faithful over a few things, I will set you over many things. Enter into the joy of your lord" (Matthew 25:14-30, WEB).

May we be those that understand that a demonstration, a gift, of the Spirit has been given to each believer and that we are expected to use that gift. These gifts are not to be used to exalt the individual, but for the building up of the church and to glorify God.

"Pursue love and desire spiritual gifts, and above all that you may prophesy." "He who prophesies builds up the church." God has given each believer a spiritual gift according to their measure of faith. "According to the grace given to us, we have different gifts." Let us be diligent to use that which has been entrusted to us that God may be glorified through all we do and say!

Chapter 12 Discussion Questions: Spiritual Gifts

1. What does it mean to prophesy, and why is it so important?
2. When two or three prophets speak, what should the others do?
3. What is to happen if something is revealed to another person sitting there?
4. According to Paul, who in the church is able to prophesy?
5. What should the expected result of prophesying be?
6. What are some of the spiritual gifts that Paul identifies in Romans and I Corinthians?
7. Paul ranks several of the gifts in order of importance. What gifts are last on the list?
8. What is the basis for the teaching that the gifts have ceased?
9. How do we know that this teaching is incorrect?
10. How do we know that there are still apostles and prophets?
11. Why are the gifts of the Spirit still needed?
12. What might be a cause of the absence of the gifts of the Spirit in Christianity today?

SECTION 3 – CONTINUING STEADFAST IN THE FAITH

THE DAY OF THE LORD

"Know this first of all, that in the last days mockers will come with their mocking, following after their own lusts, and saying, 'Where is the promise of His coming? For ever since the fathers fell asleep, all continues just as it was from the beginning of creation.'

"But do not let this one fact escape your notice, beloved, that with the Lord one day is like a thousand years, and a thousand years like one day. The Lord is not slow about His promise, as some count slowness, but is patient toward you, not wishing for any to perish but for all to come to repentance.

"But the day of the Lord will come like a thief, in which the heavens will pass away with a roar and the elements will be destroyed with intense heat, and the earth and its works will be burned up.

"Since all these things are to be destroyed in this way, what sort of people ought you to be in holy conduct and godliness, looking for and hastening the coming of the day of God, because of which the heavens will be destroyed by burning, and the elements will melt with intense heat! But according to His promise we are looking for new heavens and a new earth, in which righteousness dwells.

"Therefore, beloved, since you look for these things, be diligent to be found by Him in peace, spotless and blameless, and regard the patience of our Lord as salvation. You therefore, beloved, knowing this beforehand, be on your guard so that you are not carried away by the error of unprincipled men and fall from your own steadfastness, but grow in the grace and knowledge of our Lord and Savior Jesus Christ" (2 Peter 3:3-4, 8-18).

Notice two things are stated here concerning the day of the Lord. First, it will come like a thief. Second, this will be a day in which the heavens and the earth will be destroyed.

Jesus says in Mark 13:28-29, "Now learn the parable from the fig tree: when its branch has already become tender and puts forth its leaves, you know that summer is near. Even so, you too, when you see these things happening, recognize that He is near, right at the door." Jesus continued in verses 32-33, "But of that day or hour no one knows, not even the angels in heaven, nor the Son, but the Father alone. Take heed, keep on the alert; for you do not know when the appointed time will come."

Jesus is telling us that no one knows the time that the day of the Lord will come. However, He tells us that there will be very clear signs of its coming, so we must be alert and watchful so that day does not overtake us as a thief in the night.

Paul writes in I Thessalonians 5:1-11, "Now as to the times and the epochs, brethren, you have no need of anything to be written to you. For you yourselves know full well that the day of the Lord will come just like a thief in the night. While they are saying, 'Peace and safety!' then destruction will come upon them suddenly like labor pains upon a woman with child, and they will not escape. But you, brethren, are not in darkness, that the day would over-take you like a thief; for you are all sons of light and sons of day. For God has not destined us for wrath, but for ob-taining salvation through our Lord Jesus Christ, who died for us, so that whether we are awake or asleep, we will live together with Him. Therefore encourage one another and build up one another, just as you also are doing."

In Matthew 24:15, 21-22, Jesus tells His disciples that when they see the "ABOMINATION OF DESOLATION which was spoken of through Daniel the prophet, standing in the holy place," they need to flee and pray that their escape would not be in winter or on a Sabbath. He continues say-ing to them, "For then there will be a great tribulation, such as has not occurred since the beginning of the world until now, nor ever will. Unless those days had been cut short, no life would have been saved; but for the sake of the elect those days will be cut short."

Jesus is telling them that here is one of the signs they must be watching for, "the Abomination of Desolation spoken of through Daniel the prophet standing in the holy place." He is telling them that when they see that sign, they should be aware that a great tribulation will begin.

Paul reaffirms this warning in 2 Thessalonians 2:1, 3-4, "With regard to the coming of our Lord Jesus Christ and our gathering together to Him, let no one in any way de-ceive you, for it will not come unless the apostasy comes first, and the man of lawlessness is revealed, the son of destruction, who opposes and exalts himself above every so-called god or object of worship, so that he takes his seat in the temple of God, displaying himself as being God."

Both Paul and Jesus clearly state that the day of the Lord will not come until this event, the abomination of desolation, the man of lawlessness is revealed. Notice that the coming of our Lord and our gathering to Him will not happen until this sign takes place. When this sign happens, we are told by the Lord that then there would be the great tribulation.

Jesus continues in Matthew 24:29-31, "But immediately after the tribulation of those days THE SUN WILL BE DARKENED, AND THE MOON WILL NOT GIVE ITS LIGHT, AND THE STARS WILL FALL from the sky, and the powers of the heavens will be shaken. And then the sign of the Son of Man will appear in the sky, and then all the tribes of the earth will mourn, and they will see the SON OF MAN COMING ON THE CLOUDS OF THE SKY with power and great glory. And He will send forth His angels with A GREAT TRUMPET and THEY WILL GATHER TOGETHER His elect from the four winds, from one end of the sky to the other."

Again Paul writes in 1 Thessalonians 4:13-18 to comfort the believers saying, "But we do not want you to be uninformed, brethren, about those who are asleep, so that you will not grieve as do the rest who have no hope. For if we believe that Jesus died and rose again, even so God will bring with Him those who have fallen asleep in Jesus. For this we say to you by the word of the Lord, that we who are alive and remain until the coming of the Lord, will not precede those who have fallen asleep. For the Lord Himself will descend from heaven with a shout, with the voice of the archangel and with the trumpet of God, and the dead in Christ will rise first. Then we who are alive and remain will be caught up together with them in the clouds to meet the Lord in the air, and so we shall always be with the Lord. Therefore comfort one another with these words."

Paul writes in I Corinthians 15:52, "In a moment, in the twinkling of an eye, at the last trump: for the trumpet shall sound, and the dead shall be raised incorruptible, and we shall be changed." Here we see that the sounding of the trumpet is not just any trumpet, but the last trumpet. At the sounding of that last trumpet we, the Christians, will be changed. When is this last trumpet sounded?

The apostle John writes in Revelation 5:1,6-7, "Then I saw in the right hand of the One seated on the throne a scroll with writing on the inside and on the back, sealed with seven seals." "Then I saw One like a slaughtered lamb standing between the throne and the four living creatures and among the elders. He had seven horns and seven eyes, which are the seven spirits of God sent into all the earth. He came and took the scroll out of the right hand of the One seated on the throne" (HCSB).

Then the Lamb, our Lord Jesus Christ, began to open the seals, one by one. After He opened the sixth seal, we read in Revelation 6:17, "For the great day of His wrath has come, and who is able to stand?" (WEB). Here we see the beginning of the great and terrible day of the Lord (Joel 2:11).

When He opened the seventh seal, there was silence in heaven for about half an hour. Then John sees the seven angels who stand in the presence of God; seven trumpets were given to them. And the seven angels who had the seven trumpets prepared to blow them (Revelation 6:1-8:6).

John tells us about the first six angels as they sound their trumpets and the things that transpire (Revelation 8:1-9:21). Then John writes in Revelation 11:15, "The seventh angel sounded; and there were loud voices in heaven, saying, 'The kingdom of the world has become the kingdom of our Lord and of His Christ; and He will reign forever and ever.'" The elders say in verse 18, "The nations were angry, but Your wrath has come. The time has come for the dead to be judged, and to give the reward to Your servants the prophets, to the saints, and to those who fear Your name, both small and great, and the time has come to destroy those who destroy the earth" (HCSB).

Here we see the last seven trumpets being sounded. The last trumpet to be sounded is the seventh trumpet. It is at the sounding of this seventh trumpet that the dead will "be raised incorruptible, and we shall be changed." It is at the sound of this last trumpet that the "dead in Christ will rise first, then we who are alive and remain will be caught up together to meet the Lord in the air." It is also at the sounding of this trumpet that God will give the reward to His prophets, to the saints, and to those who fear His name, both small and great.

This is the time referred to in Matthew 24:30-31, after the great tribulation, that "they will see the SON OF MAN COMING ON THE CLOUDS OF THE SKY with power and great glory. And He will send forth His angels with A GREAT TRUMPET and THEY WILL GATHER TOGETHER His elect from the four winds, from one end of the sky to the other."

When you read the details of what happens at the opening of the first six seals and at the blowing of the seven trumpets of the seventh seal, it can be very overwhelming, even frightening. However, the Lord is always faithful to encourage and comfort His people that walk in humble obedience to Him. In Zephaniah 2:1-3, we are encouraged to, "Seek the Lord, All you humble of the earth who have carried out His ordinances; Seek righteousness, seek humility. Perhaps you will be hidden in the day of the Lord's anger."

We can also be encouraged because Jesus assures us that the time of tribulation will "be cut short" and that "for the sake of the elect those days will be cut short." Jesus also assures us of His faithful protection in Revelation 3:10

where He tells the church in Philadelphia, "Since you have kept my command to endure patiently, I will also keep you from the hour of trial that is going to come on the whole world to test the inhabitants of the earth" (NIV).

The Greek word "teros" translated as "keep" actually means "to guard". Revelation 3:10 should then be translated, "Since you have kept my command to endure patiently, I will also guard you from the hour of trial that is going to come on the whole world to test the inhabitants of the earth" (HCSB). It becomes quite apparent that it does not mean to take us out of the world to avoid going through the tribulation. It means that He will guard us, protect us, from the coming trial.

This is consistent with our Lord's prayer in John 17:15 where Jesus prays to the Father for His disciples and for those who would believe through their message saying, "I am not praying that you take them out of the world, but that You protect them from the evil one." Jesus is fully confident that the Father is able to protect those that are His.

The Bible is full of accounts of God keeping those who are faithful to Him through all kinds of trials. Hebrews 11:35-40 tells us, "Some men were tortured, not accepting release, so that they might gain a better resurrection, and others experienced mockings and scourgings, as well as bonds and imprisonment. They were stoned, they were sawed in two, they died by the sword, they wandered about in sheepskins, in goatskins, destitute, afflicted, and mistreated. The world was not worthy of them. They wandered in deserts and on mountains, hiding in caves and holes in the ground. All these were approved through their faith, but they did not receive what was promised, since God had provided something better for us, so that they would not be made perfect without us" (HCSB).

Hebrews 2:10 says, "For it was fitting for Him, for whom are all things, and through whom are all things, in bringing many sons to glory, to perfect the author of their salvation through sufferings." Again, in Hebrews 5:9, "And having been made perfect, He became to all those who obey Him the source of eternal salvation." Paul says in Colossians 1:28, "We proclaim Him (Christ), admonishing every man and teaching every man with all wisdom, so that we may present every man complete (mature, perfect) in Christ." Should we not also suffer, that we might also be brought to perfection, to maturity, in Christ?

In 2 Corinthians 13:9, Paul tells us of God's promise that "My grace is sufficient for you, for power is perfected in weakness." We have been sealed, just as the 144,000 are sealed in Revelation 7. Ephesians 1:13, says that in Christ we were sealed with the promised Holy Spirit when we believed. Ephesians 4:30 says that God's Holy Spirit sealed us for the day of redemption. Surely our God is able to guard us and watch over us through the tribulation. But even if it is His will that we die for the testimony about Jesus, we are truly blessed. We are assured that as believers, whether we live or we die, we are the Lord's.

John tells us in Revelation 20:4-6, "Then I saw thrones, and they sat on them, and judgment was given to them. And I saw the souls of those who had been beheaded because of their testimony of Jesus and because of the word of God, and those who had not worshiped the beast or his image, and had not received the mark on their forehead and on their hand; and they came to life and reigned with Christ for a thousand years. The rest of the dead did not come to life until the thousand years were completed. This is the first resurrection. Blessed and holy is the one who has a part in the first resurrection; over these the second death has no power, but they will be priests of God and of Christ and will reign with Him for a thousand years."

The tribulation and the refusal of the mark of the beast should not be things to fear if we are walking by the Spirit in obedience to the Lord, but should be a time of rejoicing for being given the opportunity to suffer for our Lord! In Acts 5:40-41, "After calling the apostles in, they flogged them and ordered them not to speak in the name of Jesus, and then released them. So they went on their way from the presence of the Council, rejoicing that they had been considered worthy to suffer shame for His name."

In Revelation 19, we see Christ defeating and capturing the beast and the false prophet and casting them alive into the lake of fire that burns with sulfur. Then, in Revelation 20, we see that an angel seized "the dragon, that ancient serpent who is the Devil and Satan, and bound him for 1,000 years." He threw him into the abyss and put a seal on it.

Then those faithful believers that were martyred, are shown ruling and reining with Christ for 1,000 years. After the 1,000 years are completed, Satan is released and goes forth and deceives the nations. Then Satan will be defeated and will be cast into the lake of fire where the beast and the false prophet are, and they will be tormented day and night forever and ever.

In Revelation 20:11-15 John writes, "Then I saw a great white throne and Him who sat upon it, from whose presence earth and heaven fled away, and no place was found for them." Then the dead, the great and the small, are judged. The books were opened; and another book was opened, which is the book of life; and the dead were judged from the things which were written in the books, according to their deeds. If anyone's name was not found written in the book of life, he was thrown into the lake of fire.

Here we see the fulfillment of Peter's prophecy that the "heavens will pass away" and "the earth and its works will be burned up." Here we see the end of the 1,000 year long "day of the Lord."

In summary, the great tribulation will take place after the abomination spoken of in Daniel is seen standing in the Holy Place. It is "immediately after" this tribulation that the Lord comes with the sound of the trumpet and the voice of the archangel and the dead in Christ rise first. Then we who are alive and remain will be gathered together to meet the Lord in the air. At the last trump, the trumpet will sound, and the dead will be raised incorruptible, and we shall be changed.

The Lord Jesus defeats the false prophet and the antichrist and casts them alive into the lake of fire, and Satan is bound and kept in the abyss for 1,000 years. The Lord rules and reigns over the earth for 1,000 years with those that come to life at the first resurrection. Then Satan is released, defeated, and cast into the lake of fire.

At the great white throne, the heaven and the earth flee from His presence. The dead are judged, and those whose names are not found in the Lamb's book of life are cast into the lake of fire. This is the end of the 1,000 year long day of the Lord, the last day, that great and terrible day of the Lord.

Four times in John 6, Jesus says that on the last day He would raise up those that believe in Him. In verse 40 Jesus says, "For this is the will of My Father: that everyone who sees the Son and believes in Him may have eternal life, and I will raise him up on the last day."

To those that have believed and taught a pretribulation rapture, I would only ask, "What if you are wrong?" What impact will it have on your faith and the faith of those you have taught if you should wake up and find that the great tribulation is taking place and all of us Christians are still here?

I fear that most believers have been taught that Christians will not have to go through such a time of suffering, and therefore, are not prepared for it. We need to be those that encourage believers to be prepared to suffer for the Lord that they may be brought to maturity in Christ.

Hebrews 5:7-9 reminds us that, "During the days of Jesus' life on earth, he offered up prayers and petitions with fervent cries and tears to the one who could save him from death, and he was heard because of his reverent submission. Son though he was, he learned obedience from what he suffered and, once made perfect, he became the source of eternal salvation for all who obey him."

Paul writes in 2 Corinthians 4:7-12, "But we have this treasure in earthen vessels, so that the surpassing greatness of the power will be of God and not from ourselves; we are afflicted in every way, but not crushed; perplexed, but not despairing; persecuted, but not forsaken; struck down, but not destroyed; always carrying about in the body the dying of Jesus, so that the life of Jesus also may be manifested in our body. For we who live are constantly being delivered over to death for Jesus' sake, so that the life of Jesus also may be manifested in our mortal flesh. So death works in us, but life in you."

He continues in verses 16-18, "Therefore we do not give up. Even though our outer man is being destroyed, our inner person is being renewed day by day. For our momentary light affliction is producing for us an absolutely incomparable eternal weight of glory. So we do not focus on what is seen, but on what is unseen. For what is seen is temporary, but what is unseen is eternal" (HCSB).

We must not let fear keep us from trusting that God will give us grace sufficient to endure whatever trial we may encounter. He uses suffering in the life of His people to bring them to maturity, to perfect them.

May we consider it a great joy whenever we experience various trials, knowing that the testing of our faith produces endurance, knowing that God is working it for our good (James 1:2).

Chapter 13 Discussion Questions: The Day of the Lord

1. What two things can we notice from 2 Peter 2 about the day of the Lord?
2. Who knows exactly when the day of the Lord will come?
3. How can we know that the end is near?
4. Why should the day of the Lord not overtake the believers like a thief in the night?
5. What sign must appear before the tribulation takes place?
6. What does Jesus say in Matthew 24 will take place when we see this sign?
7. What does Jesus say will happen immediately after the great tribulation?
8. Why is the great tribulation cut short?
9. What happens when the Lord comes with the voice of the archangel and the trumpet of God?
10. When the Lord returns, which believers will rise first?

11. What happens at the sounding of the seventh trumpet, the last trumpet?
12. What happened in Revelation 6 just before it is announced that the day of the Lord has come?
13. What does the Greek word "teros" mean in Revelation 3:10?
14. How do we know that the Lord is able to protect us through even the worst possible trials?
15. How can we know how long the day of the Lord lasts?
16. Why might there be some concern about the effect on believers of the teaching of the pre-tribulation rapture?
17. Why does God allow suffering, trials and tribulation in the life of His people?

SUFFERING FOR CHRIST

Paul encourages us in Romans 8:16-18 saying, "The Spirit Himself testifies with our spirit that we are children of God, and if children, heirs also, heirs of God and fellow heirs with Christ, if indeed we suffer with Him so that we may also be glorified with Him. For I consider that the sufferings of this present time are not worthy to be compared with the glory that is to be revealed to us."

Paul is encouraging us about the importance of suffering with Christ. We suffer with Him that we may be glorified with Him. He also reminds us that the sufferings in this life are so small and insignificant that they are not worthy to be compared with the unspeakably incredible glory that is to be revealed to us at Christ's return; if we are faithful to suffer with Him.

Philippians 1:29 tells us that God's love for us and His desire for us to grow to maturity in Christ is such that He not only granted it to us to believe, but also to suffer for His sake. "For to you it has been granted for Christ's sake, not only to believe in Him, but also to suffer for His sake." God allows us to go through times of hardship, affliction, and persecution because He loves us and He knows that these times are necessary for us to learn obedience, to learn to depend on Him and to bring us on to maturity, to complete sanctification in Christ.

It is a blessing to suffer for Christ that we might be counted worthy of the kingdom. As our sufferings for Christ are abundant, so also is His grace toward us. 2 Thessalonians 1:5 says, "This is a plain indication of God's righteous judgment so that you will be considered worthy of the kingdom of God, for which indeed you are suffering."

Paul reminds us that Christ comforts us through our afflictions. He comforts us so that we may comfort others by the same comfort that we received in Christ. 2 Corinthians 1:5-7 says, "For just as the sufferings of Christ are ours in abundance, so also our comfort is abundant through Christ. But if we are afflicted, it is for your comfort and salvation; or if we are comforted, it is for your comfort, which is effective in the patient enduring of the same sufferings which we also suffer; and our hope for you is firmly grounded, knowing that as you are sharers of our sufferings, so also you are sharers of our comfort."

God uses sufferings to perfect us, to bring us to maturity. This is the same process that God used to perfect Christ. Hebrews 2:10 tells us, "For it was fitting for Him, for whom are all things, and through whom are all things, in bringing many sons to glory, to perfect the author of their salvation through sufferings." God also uses sufferings to teach us obedience. He used sufferings in the same way with Christ. Hebrews 5:8 says, "Although He was a Son, He learned obedience from the things which He suffered."

It is pleasing to God when we bear up under the hardship and sorrow of sufferings, finding our comfort in Christ. It is pleasing to God when we patiently endure such trials, for Christ suffered for us, giving us an example of what God desires in us. I Peter 2:19-23 says, "For this finds favor, if for the sake of conscience toward God a person bears up under sorrows when suffering unjustly. For what credit is there if, when you sin and are harshly treated, you endure it with patience? But if when you do what is right and suffer for it you patiently endure it, this finds favor with God.

"For you have been called for this purpose, since Christ also suffered for you, leaving you an example for you to follow in His steps, WHO COMMITTED NO SIN, NOR WAS ANY DECEIT FOUND IN HIS MOUTH; and while being reviled, He did not revile in return; while suffering, He uttered no threats, but kept entrusting Himself to Him who judges righteously."

We need to understand that it is a blessing to suffer for the sake of righteousness. If we have this understanding, we will not grow bitter in suffering, but will rejoice that God has counted us worthy to suffer with Christ. Indeed, to be counted worthy is an incredible blessing. May we all be counted worthy of the kingdom, that we might inherit all the blessings that God has promised for those that love Him. In Acts 5:19, the apostles "went on their way from the presence of the Council, rejoicing that they had been considered worthy to suffer shame for His name."

Believers should not be surprised when they find themselves in the midst of trials. Some people teach that if a believer is having trials in their life, they must be living in sin. They teach that if a believer is walking faithfully with the Lord, they should experience health and prosperity. This, however, is not what Scripture teaches. God uses trials to test our faith and cause our faith to grow. We should rejoice in these opportunities to suffer with Christ.

I Peter 4:12-19 says, "Dear friends, do not be surprised at the fiery ordeal that has come on you to test you, as though something strange were happening to you. But rejoice inasmuch as you participate in the sufferings of Christ, so that you may be overjoyed when his glory is revealed.

"If you are insulted because of the name of Christ, you are blessed, for the Spirit of glory and of God rests on you. If you suffer, it should not be as a murderer or thief or any other kind of criminal, or even as a meddler. However, if you suffer as a Christian, do not be ashamed, but praise God that you bear that name.

"For it is time for judgment to begin with God's household; and if it begins with us, what will the outcome be for those who do not obey the gospel of God? And, 'If it is hard for the righteous to be saved, what will become of the ungodly and the sinner?' So then, those who suffer according to God's will should commit themselves to their faithful Creator and continue to do good" (NIV).

When we suffer persecution, when we suffer hardship, when we suffer various trials, we need to remember that God is in control. He will never give us more than we can endure, and He always provides us with a way of escape through His grace that is always sufficient. It is because of this grace, and His assurance through it that God loves us and works all things for our good, that we can rejoice in the midst of these trials.

It is through these sufferings, these trials, that Christ prepares us to share in His glory. He uses these trials to make us perfect, complete, lacking nothing. After we have suffered a little while He will strengthen, confirm and establish us.

God allows suffering in our lives that we may be tested. He assures us that He is in control. He tells us that He has even limited the length of time that we will suffer. He is working, even in these sufferings, for our good, that we might through them be faithful, even unto death, that we might receive from Him the crown of life. Revelation 2:10 says, "Do not fear what you are about to suffer. Behold, the devil is about to cast some of you into prison, so that you will be tested, and you will have tribulation for ten days. Be faithful until death, and I will give you the crown of life."

May the Lord enable us to praise Him, rejoicing in His goodness, while we are still in the midst of these trials. When we, by faith, rejoice in the midst of trials, we will find His grace abundantly poured out, sufficient for every trial.

Chapter 14 Discussion Questions: Suffering for Christ

1. What does Romans 8:16-18 say is contingent on our suffering with Christ?
2. What is the purpose or benefit of suffering for Christ?
3. Why is it a blessing to suffer for Christ?
4. What does 2 Thessalonians 1:5 say is a benefit of our suffering for Christ?
5. What does 2 Corinthians 1:5-7 say is a benefit of our suffering for Christ?
6. What does I Peter 2:19-23 say is pleasing to God?
7. Why are we blessed when reviled for the name of Christ?
8. Why do fiery ordeals come upon us?
9. What does I Peter 5 say will happen after we have suffered for a little while?
10. What did God promise in Revelation 2:10?

THE ELECT

Jesus told His disciples that the days of the great tribulation would be cut short for the sake of the elect. Matthew 24:20-22 says, "Pray that your flight will not be in the winter, or on a Sabbath. For then there will be a great tribulation, such as has not occurred since the beginning of the world until now, nor ever will. Unless those days had been cut short, no life would have been saved; but for the sake of the elect those days will be cut short."

Who are these "elect," and why would the Lord give them special consideration so as to even cut short the days of the great tribulation? Does the term "the elect" refer to Israel? Does it refer to the church? Is there any passage in Scripture that can give us any insight into the meaning of this term?

Romans 11:7 says, "What then? Israel did not find what it was looking for, but the elect did find it. The rest were hardened" (HCSB). Israel did not find what it was looking for, but the elect did. Obviously, Israel and the elect refer to two different things.

But how different are they? Another translation renders this verse saying, "What then? What the people of Israel sought so earnestly they did not obtain. The elect among them did, but the others were hardened" (NIV). It seems to imply that the elect, at least some of them, were a part of Israel. The elect obtained, but the rest of Israel did not obtain and were hardened. Apparently, according to this passage, the elect, at least in part, are the believing portion of the people of Israel. The rest of the people of Israel, the unbelieving portion, were hardened.

Hebrews 3:12-19 warns believers by referring to Israel and their hardening of their hearts in unbelief in the rebellion as Moses led them out of Egypt and through the wilderness. "See to it, brothers and sisters, that none of you has a sinful, unbelieving heart that turns away from the living God. But encourage one another daily, as long as it is called 'Today,' so that none of you may be hardened by sin's deceitfulness. We have come to share in Christ, if indeed we hold our original conviction firmly to the very end. As has just been said: 'Today, if you hear his voice, do not harden your hearts as you did in the rebellion.'

"Who were they who heard and rebelled? Were they not all those Moses led out of Egypt? And with whom was he angry for forty years? Was it not with those who sinned, whose bodies perished in the wilderness? And to whom did God swear that they would never enter his rest if not to those who disobeyed? So we see that they were not able to enter, because of their unbelief."

It seems clear that the elect among the children of Israel were those that believed. The rest of Israel were those whose hearts were hardened by unbelief. These unbelieving ones were the ones that rebelled, turning away from God. The question that remains is whether the elect are only the believing portion of Israel, or if the elect includes others. Is there another passage of Scripture that can more precisely identify who the elect are?

Romans 9:6-8 reminds us, "But it is not as though the word of God has failed. For they are not all Israel who are descended from Israel; nor are they all children because they are Abraham's descendants, but: 'THROUGH ISAAC YOUR DESCENDANTS WILL BE NAMED.' That is, it is not the children of the flesh who are children of God, but the children of the promise are regarded as descendants." The term "the elect" and the term "the children of promise" seem to refer to the same group of people.

Paul writes to the Gentile believers in Galatians 4:28, "And you brethren, like Isaac, are children of promise." He then writes to Timothy in 2 Timothy 2:8-13, "Remember Jesus Christ, raised from the dead, descended from David. This is my gospel, for which I am suffering even to the point of being chained like a criminal. But God's word is not chained. Therefore I endure everything for the sake of the elect, that they too may obtain the salvation that is in Christ Jesus, with eternal glory. Here is a trustworthy saying: If we died with him, we will also live with him; if we endure, we will also reign with him. If we disown him, he will also disown us; if we are faithless, he remains faithful, for he cannot disown himself."

Again, Paul writes in Titus 1:1-3, "Paul, a servant of God and an apostle of Jesus Christ to further the faith of God's elect and their knowledge of the truth that leads to godliness—in the hope of eternal life, which God, who does not lie, promised before the beginning of time, and which now at his appointed season he has brought to light through the preaching entrusted to me by the command of God our Savior." Paul states here that he endures "everything for the sake of the elect" and that the purpose of his apostleship was to "further the faith of God's elect."

I believe most people are familiar with the fact that Paul was appointed by God to be an apostle to the Gentiles. Yet here, Paul refers to those for whom he endures all things and strives to further their faith as God's elect and as the children of promise. Clearly, at least according to Paul's understanding, the Gentile believers were also the elect, the children of promise.

Peter, on the other hand was an apostle to the Jews, the circumcision. He writes in I Peter 1:1-9, "Peter, an apostle of Jesus Christ, To God's elect, exiles scattered throughout the provinces of Pontus, Galatia, Cappadocia, Asia and Bithynia, who have been chosen according to the foreknowledge of God the Father, through the sanctifying work of the Spirit, to be obedient to Jesus Christ and sprinkled with his blood: Grace and peace be yours in abundance."

Here Peter refers to these Jewish believers that he ministers to as an apostle as "God's elect." Both the Gentile believers and the Jewish believers are referred to as God's elect by the apostles of Christ. The believers, whether Jew or Gentile, are God's elect.

The elect, the children of promise, are those that live by faith. They are the spiritual descendants of Abraham who believed God and it was credited to him as righteousness. "What then shall we say that Abraham, our forefather according to the flesh, has found? For if Abraham was justified by works, he has something to boast about, but not before God. For what does the Scripture say? 'ABRAHAM BELIEVED GOD, AND IT WAS CREDITED TO HIM AS RIGHTEOUSNESS.' Now to the one who works, his wage is not credited as a favor, but as what is due. But to the one who does not work, but believes in Him who justifies the ungodly, his faith is credited as righteousness" (Romans 4:1-5).

The elect, the children of promise, are those that do not seek a righteousness of their own that comes through the law, but the righteousness of God through faith in Jesus Christ. Romans 3:21-22 says, "But now apart from the Law the righteousness of God has been manifested, being witnessed by the Law and the Prophets, even the righteousness of God through faith in Jesus Christ for all those who believe."

From these passages we see that the days of the tribulation were cut short, not for the descendants of Israel according to the flesh, but for the spiritual descendants of Israel, the children of promise. The time was cut short for the people of faith. It was cut short for those whose faith was credited to them as righteousness, the righteousness of God through faith in Jesus Christ. The time of the great tribulation will be cut short for the sake of the elect, the believers, both Jew and Gentile, the church.

The great tribulation will be cut short for their sake because the church will be here on the earth throughout the great tribulation. As we saw in the previous chapter, immediately after the great tribulation, the Lord will descend from heaven with a shout, with the voice of the archangel and with the trumpet of God, and the dead in Christ will rise first. Then we who are alive and remain will be caught up together with them in the clouds to meet the Lord in the air. The Lord will send forth His angels with a great trumpet and they will gather together His elect from the four winds, from one end of the sky to the other.

The fact that the days of the great tribulation will be cut short for the sake of the elect demonstrates God's unceasing care for His people. This is consistent with the promise made in Revelation 3:10 where Jesus says, "Since you have kept my command to endure patiently, I will also guard you from the hour of trial that is going to come on the whole world to test the inhabitants of the earth" (HCSB).

The great and terrible day of the Lord will be a horrifying day of judgment on the world and upon those that hate God and have rebelled against Him and have steadfastly refused to repent that they might not perish. However, for the elect the day of the Lord will be a time of joyful anticipation of the fulfillment of all the promises of God handed down through the apostles and prophets. Paul writes in 2 Timothy 4:8, "In the future there is laid up for me the crown of righteousness, which the Lord, the righteous Judge, will award to me on that day; and not only to me, but also to all who have loved His appearing." It will be a time of God's judgment on His enemies and of rewards for His faithful servants.

The days of the great tribulation will be cut short for the sake of the elect. The day of the Lord will be for the fulfillment of all of God's promises to His people, the children of promise, the elect, and for the judgment of the rebellious and the disobedient. It will be the time of His wrath and His reward.

Chapter 15 Discussion Questions: The Elect

1. Why will the days of the great tribulation be cut short?
2. How do we know the "the elect" in Matthew 24 does not refer to Israel?
3. Who does Romans 11:7 say did not obtain what they were looking for?
4. Who does Romans 11:7 say did obtain it?

5. What part, if any, of the children of Israel obtained what they were looking for?

6. According to Hebrews 3, who hardened their hearts in the rebellion in the wilderness?

7. In Hebrews 3, what are we warned about that can harden our hearts?

8. Who does Romans 9:6-8 say are and are not the children of God?

9. How do we know that the Gentile believers are the elect, the children of promise?

10. How do we know that the Jewish believers are the elect?

11. What righteousness do the elect seek?

12. What sign must take place before the great tribulation?

13. What does Jesus say will happen immediately after the great tribulation?

14. What happens when Christ returns and the trumpet sounds?

15. Who is the crown of righteousness laid up for?

CALLED AND CHOSEN AND FAITHFUL

"These will wage war against the Lamb, and the Lamb will overcome them, because He is Lord of lords and King of kings, and those who are with Him are the called and chosen and faithful" (Revelation 17:14).

The Greek word "eklektos" that is translated as "chosen" in this verse is the same Greek word that is translated as "elect" in Matthew 24:24. It means selected. As we have previously seen, this word is used to refer to the people of faith, the children of promise, the church. It is also the same word that is translated as "chosen" in Matthew 22:14, where it says, "Many are called, but few are chosen."

The word "called" in this verse means "invited." God desires that none would perish (2 Peter 3:9). He has therefore, time and time again, called for people to repent and turn back to Him. "The LORD sent all His servants the prophets to you time and time again, but you have not obeyed or even paid attention. He announced, 'Turn, each of you, from your evil way of life and from your evil deeds'" (Jeremiah 25:4-5, HCSB).

God even sent His only Son, Jesus, to call people to repent, and through Him to return to God. Jesus said in Matthew 11:28, "Come to Me, all who are weary and heavy-laden, and I will give you rest." This invitation was directed to "all," to any that were weary. Again, Jesus offered the invitation in John 7:37-38 saying, "If anyone is thirsty, let him come to Me and drink. He who believes in Me, as the Scripture said, 'From his innermost being will flow rivers of living water.'" Finally, in Revelation 22:17, "The Spirit and the bride say, 'Come!' He who hears, let him say, 'Come!' He who is thirsty, let him come. He who desires, let him take the water of life freely" (WEB).

Paul writes in Romans 10:18, "Their voice has gone out into all the earth, their words to the ends of the world." He is referring to the gospel message offering salvation to all who will repent and come to God through faith in Jesus Christ. These are the called, everyone to whom God has offered the free gift of eternal life through faith in Jesus Christ.

The ones that respond to this call, this invitation, by faith, are the elect, the chosen. The ones that respond by faith to the gospel message are selected by God to receive His free gift of eternal life through Jesus Christ the Lord.

Matthew 22:14 says, "For many are called, but few are chosen." The called in this verse are all those to whom the offer of salvation through faith in Christ has been extended. They have been invited. The chosen are the few that have accepted the invitation and have come by faith to Christ. They have been selected by God to be His people.

So we return to Revelation 17:14 and consider again, who are these that are with Christ that are referred to as called, chosen, and faithful? We have identified the called, and we have identified the chosen. But who are the faithful?

In Revelation chapters 2 and 3, Jesus sends a letter to each of seven churches. He ends each letter with a promise to the victorious Christians, to those that overcome every trial and persevere, enduring to the end. They are the ones that remain steadfast in their faith and are faithfully and joyfully waiting for the return, the appearing of their Lord, Jesus Christ.

To the church in Ephesus He says, "I will give the victor the right to eat from the tree of life." To the church in Smyrna He says, "The victor will never be harmed by the second death." To the church in Pergamum He says, "I will give the victor some of the hidden manna." To the church in Thyatira He says, "The victor and the one who keeps My works to the end: I will give him authority over the nations." To the church in Sardis He says, "The victor will be dressed in white clothes, and I will never erase his name from the book of life, but will acknowledge his name before My Father and before His angels." To the church in Philadelphia He says, "The victor: I will make him a pillar in the sanctuary of My God." To the church In Laodicea He says, "The victor: I will give him the right to sit with Me on My throne, just as I also won the victory and sat down with My Father on His throne" (HCSB).

John observes in Revelation 20:4-6, "Then I saw thrones, and they sat on them, and judgment was given to them. And I saw the souls of those who had been beheaded because of their testimony of Jesus and because of the word of God, and those who had not worshiped the beast or his image, and had not received the mark on their forehead and on their hand; and they came to life and reigned with Christ for a thousand years. The rest of the dead did not come to life until the thousand years were completed. This is the first resurrection. Blessed and holy is the one who has a part in the first resurrection; over these the second death has no power, but they will be priests of God and of Christ and will reign with Him for a thousand years." These that have attained unto the first resurrection will rule and reign with Christ. These have faithfully endured unto the end, suffering with Christ, even to the point of death. The word translated as "first" in this passage means "foremost" in time, place, order, or importance. It means first or best.

Paul writes longingly in Philippians 3:10-15, "That I may know Him and the power of His resurrection and the fellowship of His sufferings, being conformed to His death; in order that I may attain to the resurrection from the dead. Not that I have already obtained it or have already become perfect, but I press on so that I may lay hold of that for which also I was laid hold of by Christ Jesus. Brethren, I do not regard myself as having laid hold of it yet; but one thing I do: forgetting what lies behind and reaching forward to what lies ahead, I press on toward the goal for the prize of the upward call of God in Christ Jesus. Let us therefore, as many as are perfect, have this attitude."

Paul's goal was to attain unto this first, best, resurrection. This was the purpose for which he was laid hold of by Christ. Christ desires that all the chosen would be faithful. This should also be our goal.

The faithful are the ones that have endured to the end and could say with Paul, "For I am already being poured out as a drink offering, and the time of my departure has come. I have fought the good fight, I have finished the course, I have kept the faith; in the future there is laid up for me the crown of righteousness, which the Lord, the righteous Judge, will award to me on that day; and not only to me, but also to all who have loved His appearing" (2 Timothy 4:6-8).

A crown indicates royalty. It indicates one that will rule and reign. It reminds us that we are to be a royal priesthood. "But you are a chosen people, a royal priesthood, a holy nation, God's special possession, that you may declare the praises of him who called you out of darkness into his wonderful light" (1 Peter 2:9, NIV).

Hebrews 11 rehearses the lives and the works of God's people that endured every manner of trial and temptation and became heirs of the righteousness that comes by faith. By faith, through obedience, they pleased God. Verse 39 says, "And all these, having gained approval through their faith, did not receive what was promised, because God had provided something better for us, so that apart from us they would not be made perfect." These sought something better. They sought the fulfillment of the heavenly promise, and they would not be satisfied with earthly treasures.

All of these passages refer to the "faithful" that are with Christ in Revelation 17:14 and in Revelation 20:1-6. These are the ones that are called and chosen and faithful. These all sought an eternity of ruling and reigning with Christ, rejoicing in God's glorious presence. They sought to attain unto that for which they were called and chosen. They were faithful.

So, who are the ones that are called, and chosen, but not faithful? In Matthew 25, Jesus is sitting on the Mount of Olives speaking to His disciples about the end times and the kingdom of heaven. He tells them a parable about the talents. He said it is like a man about to go on a journey, who called his own slaves and entrusted his possessions to them. To one he gave five talents. To another he gave two talents. And to the third slave he gave one talent. He gave to each one according to their ability.

When the master returned from his journey, he settled accounts with each of the slaves. The one with the five talents had earned five more. The master said to him, "Well done, good and faithful slave. You were faithful with a few things, I will put you in charge of many things; enter into the joy of your master." The one with two talents had earned two more talents. The master said to him, "Well done, good and faithful slave. You were faithful with a few things, I will put you in charge of many things; enter into the joy of your master."

The one with the one talent said, "I was afraid, and went away and hid your talent in the ground. See, you have what is yours." His master said to him, 'You wicked, lazy slave." Then the master said, "Take away the talent from him, and give it to the one who has the ten talents. For to everyone who has, more shall be given, and he will have an abundance; but from the one who does not have, even what he does have shall be taken away. Throw out the worthless slave into the outer darkness; in that place there will be weeping and gnashing of teeth." The Greek word "exoteros" translated as "outer" means exterior. The Greek word "skotos" translated as "darkness" means shadiness.

Notice that the slaves that used what their master had entrusted to them to gain more for their master were referred to by their master as faithful. The slave that was afraid, produced no fruit and gained nothing for his master from all that was entrusted to him, was referred to by his master as wicked, lazy and worthless. His time and his talents had been wasted.

This is similar to the parable of the sower in Matthew 13:20-23. "The one on whom seed was sown on the rocky places, this is the man who hears the word and immediately receives it with joy; yet he has no firm root in himself, but is only temporary, and when affliction or persecution arises because of the word, immediately he falls away. And the one on whom seed was sown among the thorns, this is the man who hears the word, and the worry of the world and the deceitfulness of wealth choke the word, and it becomes unfruitful. And the one on whom seed was sown on the good soil, this is the man who hears the word and understands it; who indeed bears fruit and brings forth, some a hundredfold, some sixty, and some thirty."

The one that hears the word and understands it bears much fruit. The others that hear the word and receive it joyfully produce no fruit because they are overcome by persecution or affliction, or they are distracted by the worries of the world and the deceitfulness of riches that choke off the word. Having failed to understand the word and therefore having failed to value the word, these were not steadfast in their faith. They had no root and they lost their focus on what was important.

The faithful were ushered into the joy of their master. They were faithful over a few things and were therefore put in charge of many things. They will rule and reign with their master. This is like the ones in the first resurrection in Revelation 20 that ruled and reigned with Christ for 1,000 years. This is also like the ones that rule and reign with God for eternity in the New Jerusalem in Revelation 22:1-5.

The unfaithful are cast into outer darkness where there will be weeping and gnashing of teeth. This could be like the one that was not allowed in to partake of the wedding feast in Matthew 22:1-13. When the king came in to view the guests, he saw one that did not have on a wedding garment. The king ordered that the guest that was not properly dressed be bound hand and foot and cast out into outer darkness where there was weeping and gnashing of teeth.

Revelation 19:7-9 says, "'Let us rejoice and be glad and give the glory to Him, for the marriage of the Lamb has come and His bride has made herself ready.' It was given to her to clothe herself in fine linen, bright and clean; for the fine linen is the righteous acts of the saints. Then he said to me, 'Write, "Blessed are those who are invited to the marriage supper of the Lamb."'"

The righteous acts of the saints, refers to them having ceased from their own works and having rested in the finished work of Christ, being justified by the blood that He shed for them. It refers to them working in obedience to the leading of Christ as the indwelling Spirit empowering them to do everything that God required of them. It refers to them loving one another as Christ had loved them.

As Christians, we must understand that we will be judged by how we live this life, whether walking according to the Spirit, or walking according to the lusts of the flesh. Are we abiding in Christ, walking as He walked (1John 2:6)? Are we holy as He is holy (1 Peter 1:16)? The Spirit is given to born-again believers to enable them to live holy lives and to walk as Jesus walked, in full obedience to the Father.

Our eternal destiny will depend on whether we walk in faithful obedience to the Lord and endure all hardship for His sake and for His glory. If we continue steadfast in the faith, we will receive that crown of righteousness. If we endure trials joyfully as an opportunity to learn obedience and to grow unto maturity in Christ, remaining faithful unto the end, we will receive that crown of righteousness.

However, if we are unfaithful, we will suffer great loss. If we allow persecution and affliction to discourage us from walking in obedience to the Lord, we will be considered wicked, lazy and unfaithful servants. If we allow the cares of this life and the deceitfulness of wealth to choke off the word that has been entrusted to us, we will be considered wicked, lazy and unfaithful servants. We will be as the unfruitful slave that was cast into outer darkness, where there will be weeping and gnashing of teeth.

"For no man can lay a foundation other than the one which is laid, which is Jesus Christ. Now if any man builds on the foundation with gold, silver, precious stones, wood, hay, straw, each man's work will become evident; for the day will show it because it is to be revealed with fire, and the fire itself will test the quality of each man's work. If any man's work which he has built on it remains, he will receive a reward. If any man's work is burned up, he will suffer loss; but he himself will be saved, yet so as through fire" (I Corinthians 3:11-15).

If we walk according to the flesh, serving the Lord in our own strength, according to our own understanding, we will be like those in I Corinthians 3 that built with wood, hay, and straw. At the judgment, their works were destroyed, burned up, yet they were saved as through fire. They did not receive a reward, but rather they suffered great loss.

2 Peter 3:7 says, "But the heavens that exist now and the earth, by the same word have been stored up for fire, being reserved against the day of judgment and destruction of ungodly men." Verses 10-12 continue, "But the day of the Lord will come as a thief in the night; in which the heavens will pass away with a great noise, and the elements will be dissolved with fervent heat, and the earth

and the works that are in it will be burned up. Therefore since all these things will be destroyed like this, what kind of people ought you to be in holy living and godliness, looking for and earnestly desiring the coming of the day of God, which will cause the burning heavens to be dissolved, and the elements will melt with fervent heat? But, according to his promise, we look for new heavens and a new earth, in which righteousness dwells."

Revelation 21 and 22 reveals that John sees the city, New Jerusalem, coming down from the new heavens to the new earth. The New Jerusalem is adorned as a bride prepared for her husband. It is revealed that God's dwelling place will be in the New Jerusalem. John says in 21:3-4, "I heard a loud voice from the throne, saying, "Behold, the tabernacle of God is among men, and He will dwell among them, and they shall be His people, and God Himself will be among them, and He will wipe away every tear from their eyes; and there will no longer be any death; there will no longer be any mourning, or crying, or pain; the first things have passed away."

"Those who are victorious will inherit all this, and I will be their God and they will be my children" (Revelation 21:7, NIV). The victorious will inherit the New Jerusalem with all of its blessings. The victorious elect will inherit all the promises of God, all the promises that God has made through His apostles and prophets to the children of promise.

Verse 24 says that the nations will walk in the light of the New Jerusalem. The kings of the earth will bring the glory and honor of the nations into the New Jerusalem. The leaves of the tree of life will be for the healing of the nations. Isaiah 66:22-24 says that the nations will come to the New Jerusalem to worship the Lord. As they leave, they will see the lake of fire, a memorial of God's righteous judgment where they will see the corpses, the dead bodies of those that rebelled against the Lord. Revelation 21:7-8 says, "It is done! I am Alpha and Omega, the beginning and the end. I will give to the thirsty water without price from the fountain of life. The victorious shall inherit these things, and I will be God to him and he will be son to Me. But as for the cowards, the faithless and the corrupt, the murderers, the traffickers in sex and sorcery, the worshippers of idols and all liars—their inheritance is in the lake which burns with fire and sulphur, which is the second death" (Phillips).

Three places are recorded as being on the new earth. The city of New Jerusalem adorned as a bride for her husband, will be the inheritance of the faithful, the victorious Christians, the children of promise, the Jewish and Gentile people of faith in Christ from every age or era.

Outside the city will be the lake of fire with the corpses of the rebellious as a memorial of God's righteous judgment. Also, outside the city will be the outer darkness, the exterior area of shadiness. This place of shadow outside the city is where the nations will live.

Those that are not faithful to use what was entrusted to them for the building up of the church and for the glory of God may find that their eternal destiny is not within the New Jerusalem, but outside of it. Isaiah 65:17-19 says, "For, behold, I create new heavens and a new earth; and the former things will not be remembered, nor come into mind. But be glad and rejoice forever in that which I create; for, behold, I create Jerusalem to be a delight, and her people a joy. I will rejoice in Jerusalem, and delight in my people; and the voice of weeping and the voice of crying will be heard in her no more."

Verses 20-22 reveal the life of those outside of the New Jerusalem saying, "No more will there be an infant who only lives a few days, nor an old man who has not filled his days; for the child will die one hundred years old, and the sinner being one hundred years old will be accursed. They will build houses and inhabit them. They will plant vineyards and eat their fruit. They will not build and another inhabit. They will not plant and another eat" (WEB). We know that this is not speaking of those inside the New Jerusalem because Revelation 21:4, speaking of the New Jerusalem says, "Death will be no more."

May we all continue steadfast in our faith and endure to the end. Let us consider one another as better than ourselves. Let us commit ourselves to using that which has been entrusted to us, the life of Christ as the Spirit within our spirit, and the gifts of the Spirit, to build the church and to glorify God in all we say and do. May our desire be for every believer to arrive at the unity of the faith and to attain unto maturity, growing together into the fulness of the stature of Christ.

"Therefore, brothers and sisters, since we have confidence to enter the Most Holy Place by the blood of Jesus, by a new and living way opened for us through the curtain, that is, his body, and since we have a great priest over the house of God, let us draw near to God with a sincere heart and with the full assurance that faith brings, having our hearts sprinkled to cleanse us from a guilty conscience and having our bodies washed with pure water. Let us hold unswervingly to the hope we profess, for he who promised is faithful. And let us consider how we may spur one another on toward love and good deeds, not giving up meeting together, as some are in the habit of doing, but encouraging one another—and all the more as you see the Day approaching" (Hebrews 10:19-25, NIV).

May we all be victorious Christians!

Chapter 16 Discussion Questions: Called and Chosen and Faithful

1. Who will be with the Lamb as he overcomes those that make war with Him?
2. Who are the called?
3. Who are the chosen?
4. Why does God invite everyone to repent and turn in faith to Jesus?
5. Who are the faithful?
6. Who came to life in the first resurrection and reigned with Christ 1,000 years?
7. What resurrection did Paul desire to attain unto?
8. Who are the ones that are the called and chosen and unfaithful?
9. In the parable of the talents, what did the master say to the faithful slaves?
10. What did the master say about the slave that was afraid and produced nothing?
11. In the parable of the sower, what is the difference between the one that bears fruit and the others?
12. Where are the unfruitful and the ones without the wedding garment cast?
13. As Christians, what will determine our eternal destiny?
14. What are the three areas revealed in Revelation 21 and 22 as being on the new earth?
15. Who will inherit the blessings of living in the New Jerusalem?
16. Where will the nations be?

17. Where will the lake of fire be?
18. What is your goal as a Christian?
19. What do you have to do to be a victorious Christian?

THE KINDNESS AND SEVERITY OF GOD

Many Christians have the idea that once you are born again, your destiny is assured, and when you die or when the Lord returns, you will go to heaven and spend eternity in the Lord's presence in the kingdom of God. Many seem to think that what they do between being born again and when they go to meet the Lord is not really that important. But what do the Scriptures say?

In Romans 11, Paul writes to the believers in Rome warning them not to be conceited, or arrogant. He reminds them of how some of the natural olive branches, the children of Israel, were broken off from the natural olive tree because of their unbelief. These natural branches were broken off that we, the Gentiles, the wild olive branches, might be grafted in.

He warned that we need to fear that if God broke off the natural branches because of their unbelief, He will break us off if we fail to continue steadfast in the faith. To those that continue to stand firm in their faith, God reveals His kindness. To those that fall into unbelief and disobedience, God reveals His severity. If God did not spare the natural branches, you can be sure He will not spare us if we are disobedient and unfaithful.

Romans 11:17-22 says, "But if some of the branches were broken off, and you, being a wild olive, were grafted in among them and became partaker with them of the rich root of the olive tree, do not be arrogant toward the branches; but if you are arrogant, remember that it is not you who supports the root, but the root supports you. You will say then, 'Branches were broken off so that I might be grafted in.' Quite right, they were broken off for their unbelief, but you stand by your faith. Do not be conceited, but fear; for if God did not spare the natural branches, He will not spare you, either. Behold then the kindness and severity of God; to those who fell, severity, but to you, God's kindness, if you continue in His kindness; otherwise you also will be cut off."

Jesus said in John 15:4-11 "Abide in Me, and I in you. As the branch cannot bear fruit of itself unless it abides in the vine, so neither can you unless you abide in Me. I am the vine, you are the branches; he who abides in Me and I in him, he bears much fruit, for apart from Me you can do nothing. If anyone does not abide in Me, he is thrown away as a branch and dries up; and they gather them, and cast them into the fire and they are burned. If you abide in Me, and My words abide in you, ask whatever you wish, and it will be done for you. My Father is glorified by this, that you bear much fruit, and so prove to be My disciples. Just as the Father has loved Me, I have also loved you; abide in My love. If you keep My commandments, you will abide in My love; just as I have kept My Father's commandments and abide in His love. These things I have spoken to you so that My joy may be in you, and that your joy may be made full."

Notice that Jesus says that if we abide, or remain, in Him, He will abide, or remain, in us. He said that if anyone does not remain in Him, that person would be cut off as a branch and is cast into the fire and is burned. However, He says if we remain in Him, we will bear much fruit. If we keep His commandments, we will remain in His love. According to Jesus, our destiny is contingent on whether we are faithful to remain in Him. If we are disobedient and unfaithful, He will break us off as branches, just as Paul warned, and cast us into the fire to be burned.

Paul, in Colossians 1:21-23, tells the believers in Colossae, that Christ reconciled you through His death, "in order to present you before Him holy and blameless and beyond reproach—if indeed you continue in the faith firmly established and steadfast, and not moved away from the hope of the gospel that you have heard, which was proclaimed in all creation under heaven." Notice again the contingency here. We will be presented before Him holy and blameless and beyond reproach, if. If what? If we continue in the faith, firmly established and not moved away from the hope of the gospel.

Paul again writes in 2 Timothy 2:10-13, "For this reason I endure all things for the sake of those who are chosen, so that they also may obtain the salvation which is in Christ Jesus and with it eternal glory. It is a trustworthy statement: For if we died with Him, we will also live with Him; If we endure, we will also reign with Him; If we deny Him, He also will deny us; If we are faithless, He remains faithful, for He cannot deny Himself."

He makes it very clear that, as believers, our destiny is very much dependent on our actions. Paul endured all things for the sake of the elect, the chosen, so they also may obtain the salvation which is in Christ Jesus and with it eternal glory. Paul had seen that there was much more to believing in Jesus than just being born again.

It was for this goal, this desire to attain unto this full salvation that was available in Christ Jesus, that He was pressing toward in Philippians 3:12-13. "Not that I have already obtained it or have already become perfect, but I press on so that I may lay hold of that for which also I was laid hold of by Christ Jesus. Brethren, I do not regard myself as having laid hold of it yet; but one thing I do: forgetting what lies behind and reaching forward to what lies ahead."

It was for this goal that he endured all things for the sake of the elect. He desired that the elect would attain unto, would obtain, this full salvation; which is in Christ Jesus, and with it eternal glory.

He did not want the elect to miss out on all that was available to them in Christ. Therefore, he reminded them, if we died with Him, we will also live with Him; If we endure, we will also reign with Him. He was also warning them that if we deny Him, He will deny us. He wanted them to understand that if we are faithless, He remains faithful, for He cannot deny Himself.

Some Christians seem to think that, "if we are faithless, He remains faithful, for He cannot deny Himself," means that no matter how we live, God will take care of everything and make sure we make it safely to heaven to spend eternity with Him. This is not at all what it means. "He remains faithful, for He cannot deny Himself," means that He is going to keep His word. He is going to be faithful to do exactly what He has promised. If we are unfaithful, He will remain faithful to His word; He will cut us off. If we deny Him, He will be faithful to keep His word; He will deny us. He cannot deny Himself. He must fulfill His promise.

Deuteronomy 30:15-20 says, "See, I have set before you today life and prosperity, and death and adversity; in that I command you today to love the LORD your God, to walk in His ways and to keep His commandments and His statutes and His judgments, that you may live and multiply, and that the LORD your God may bless you in the land where you are entering to possess it. But if your heart turns away and you will not obey, but are drawn away and worship other gods and serve them, I declare to you today that you shall surely perish. You will not prolong your days in the land where you are crossing the Jordan to enter and possess it. I call heaven and earth to witness against you today, that I have set before you life and death, the blessing and the curse. So choose life in order that you may live, you and your descendants, by loving the LORD your God, by obeying His voice, and by holding fast to Him."

In Galatians 6:7-10, Paul makes it very clear, "Do not be deceived, God is not mocked; for whatever a man sows, this he will also reap. For the one who sows to his own flesh will from the flesh reap corruption, but the one who sows to the Spirit will from the Spirit reap eternal life. Let us not lose heart in doing good, for in due time we will reap if we do not grow weary. So then, while we have opportunity, let us do good to all people, and especially to those who are of the household of the faith." You do not want to mess with God. He takes His word, His promises, very seriously. He has every intention of doing exactly what He promised He would do. He is not a respecter of persons; He is a respecter of the integrity of His word.

Our confidence must not be in our faith, but rather in God's faithfulness. Our faith may waver, our faith may be weak, but God remains faithful. To say that God remains faithful does not mean that even if we are faithless and deny God and choose to walk according to the flesh, that it is okay with God because He will be faithful to give us everything He promised anyway. No, for God to remain faithful means simply that God will keep His word. What He has said, He will do. Our disobedience will not change God's faithfulness. Whether we remain faithful or not will have no effect on God's faithfulness. God will still keep His word. God will continue to be faithful to fulfill what He has promised.

If we are faithful and obedient, we will experience God's kindness. If we are disobedient and unfaithful, we will experience God's severity and righteous judgment.

In Hebrews 10:26-39, the writer stresses this point again saying, "If we deliberately keep on sinning after we have received the knowledge of the truth, no sacrifice for sins is left, but only a fearful expectation of judgment and of raging fire that will consume the enemies of God. Anyone who rejected the law of Moses died without mercy on the testimony of two or three witnesses. How much more severely do you think someone deserves to be punished who has trampled the Son of God underfoot, who has treated as an unholy thing the blood of the covenant that sanctified them, and who has insulted the Spirit of grace? For we know him who said, 'It is mine to avenge; I will repay,' and again, 'The Lord will judge his people.'

"It is a dreadful thing to fall into the hands of the living God. Remember those earlier days after you had received the light, when you endured in a great conflict full of suffering. Sometimes you were publicly exposed to insult and persecution; at other times you stood side by side with those who were so treated. You suffered along with those in prison and joyfully accepted the confiscation of your property, because you knew that you yourselves had better and lasting possessions.

"So do not throw away your confidence; it will be richly rewarded. You need to persevere so that when you have done the will of God, you will receive what he has promised. For, 'In just a little while, he who is coming will come and will not delay.' And, 'But my righteous one will live by faith. And I take no pleasure in the one who shrinks back.' But we do not belong to those who shrink back and are destroyed, but to those who have faith and are saved."

Jesus says in Matthew 10:37-39, "He who loves father or mother more than Me is not worthy of Me; and he who loves son or daughter more than Me is not worthy of Me. And he who does not take his cross and follow after Me is not worthy of Me. He who has found his life will lose it, and he who has lost his life for My sake will find it." Jesus expects, yes, He demands the preeminence, the first place, in the believer's life. He will settle for nothing less.

Jesus tells His disciples this parable in Matthew 13:17-23, "Hear then the parable of the sower. When anyone hears the word of the kingdom and does not understand it, the evil one comes and snatches away what has been sown in his heart. This is the one on whom seed was sown beside the road.

"The one on whom seed was sown on the rocky places, this is the man who hears the word and immediately receives it with joy; yet he has no firm root in himself, but is only temporary, and when affliction or persecution arises because of the word, immediately he falls away. And the one on whom seed was sown among the thorns, this is the man who hears the word, and the worry of the world and the deceitfulness of wealth choke the word, and it becomes unfruitful. And the one on whom seed was sown on the good soil, this is the man who hears the word and understands it; who indeed bears fruit and brings forth, some a hundredfold, some sixty, and some thirty."

Notice that Jesus mentions four things that can keep a believer from bearing fruit. Affliction, persecution, the worry of the world, and the deceitfulness of wealth can choke the word, and it becomes unfruitful. We need to be on guard. We need to be watchful, lest any of these things causes the word in us to be unfruitful. We are also warned in I John 2:15, "Do not love the world nor the things in the world. If anyone loves the world, the love of the Father is not in him."

Jesus tells us in Matthew 6:24, "No one can serve two masters; for either he will hate the one and love the other, or he will be devoted to one and despise the other. You cannot serve God and wealth.

"For this reason I say to you, do not be worried about your life, as to what you will eat or what you will drink; nor for your body, as to what you will put on. Is not life more than food, and the body more than clothing? Look at the birds of the air, that they do not sow, nor reap nor gather into barns, and yet your heavenly Father feeds them. Are you not worth much more than they?"

We need to be careful not to be seduced by the deceitfulness of riches or be drawn away by a love of the world or the things of the world. We must continually guard our heart. We must continually reaffirm that Jesus Christ our Lord is really our Lord and is the most precious thing in our life.

Again, Jesus says in Mark 8:34-38, "And He summoned the crowd with His disciples, and said to them, 'If anyone wishes to come after Me, he must deny himself, and take up his cross and follow Me. For whoever wishes to save his life will lose it, but whoever loses his life for My sake and the gospel's will save it. For what does it profit a man to gain the whole world, and forfeit his soul? For what will a man give in exchange for his soul? For whoever is ashamed of Me and My words in this adulterous and sinful generation, the Son of Man will also be ashamed of him when He comes in the glory of His Father with the holy angels.'"

In I Corinthians 15:1-2 Paul writes, "Now I make known to you, brethren, the gospel which I preached to you, which also you received, in which also you stand, by which also you are saved, if you hold fast the word which I preached to you, unless you believed in vain." Paul reminds them that they heard and received the gospel in which they stand and by which they are saved, if they hold fast to it, unless they believed in vain.

In Acts 14:21-22, Paul encourages the believers to continue in the faith saying, "Through many tribulations we must enter the kingdom of God." We need to understand that there will be trials, there will be difficult times; but if in the midst of them, we remain faithful and steadfast in our faith, God will remain faithful to keep His word and grant us grace sufficient for every situation.

Hebrews 12:14-17 says, "Pursue peace with all men, and the sanctification without which no one will see the Lord. See to it that no one comes short of the grace of God; that no root of bitterness springing up causes trouble, and by it many be defiled; that there be no immoral or godless person like Esau, who sold his own birthright for a single meal. For you know that even afterwards, when he desired to inherit the blessing, he was rejected, for he found no place for repentance, though he sought for it with tears."

Let us not be those that, like Esau, despise our birthright. Rather, let us be those that understand the importance of valuing the birthright of every believer, our inheritance of the promises of God.

God has promised blessings upon those that remain faithful, for those that obey Him. God has promised cursings upon those that are unfaithful, for those that rebel against Him. If we do not continue faithful and endure to the end, we will not inherit the blessings, but God will faithfully bring judgement upon us just as He promised. If we continue faithful and endure to the end, we will inherit the blessings just as God has promised.

God remains faithful. God spoke to Abraham, and Abraham believed Him and it was counted as righteousness to him. We need to believe God because He is faithful. Whatever He promises, He will do. God, in His kindness and mercy, has saved us and grafted us into the true vine. God, in His severity and righteousness, will cut us off because of our unbelief. We stand by faith; but we will be cut off if we fall into unbelief.

May we each endure to the end, loving nothing or no one more than our Lord Jesus Christ, that we might reign with Him and inherit all the blessings that God has promised to the faithful and the victorious!

Chapter 17 Discussion Questions: The Kindness and Severity of God

1. Why does Paul warn us in Romans 11 not to be conceited?
2. What does he say we need to fear?
3. What did Jesus say in John 15 would happen if we do not abide in Him?

4. What did Paul tell the Colossians was the reason that Christ reconciled them?

5. What did Paul tell Timothy will happen if we faithfully endure?

6. What did Paul mean when he said, "If we are faithless, He remains faithful, for He cannot deny Himself"?

7. What did God set before the children of Israel in Deuteronomy 30?

8. What did Paul mean in Galatians 6 when he said God is not mocked?

9. What happens if we deliberately keep on sinning after receiving a knowledge of the truth?

10. Why does Jesus say, "He who loves father or mother more than Me is not worthy of Me"?

11. What does it mean to believe in vain?

INHERITING THE PROMISES

When God created man, He formed him from the dust of the ground, and breathed into his nostrils the breath of life, and man became a living soul. Then God prepared a garden for the man to care for. God caused every tree that was beautiful in appearance and good for food to grow in the garden. In the midst of the garden, God caused the tree of life to grow, as well as the tree of knowledge of good and evil.

"The LORD God took the man and put him in the Garden of Eden to work it and take care of it. And the LORD God commanded the man, 'You are free to eat from any tree in the garden; but you must not eat from the tree of the knowledge of good and evil, for when you eat from it you will certainly die'" (Genesis 2:15-17).

This was God's first promise to man. If the man would obey God and not eat from the fruit of the tree of the knowledge of good and evil, man would have the opportunity and the right to eat of the tree of life. God made the tree of life available for man to freely eat from, as well as from any other tree in the garden. God's only requirement was that the man not eat from the tree of the knowledge of good and evil.

Before the man could eat of the tree of life, Satan, the serpent, came and spoke to the man's wife and deceived her into believing that the fruit of the tree of the knowledge of good and evil was actually good to eat. He convinced her that God was not good and was withholding the best from them because He did not want them to become wise like God Himself, knowing good and evil.

After the man's wife had become deceived and had eaten of the fruit of the tree of the knowledge of good and evil, she gave some to her husband and he ate of it. After man rebelled by disobeying God's commandment not to eat of the tree of the knowledge of good and evil, God intervened and stopped the man and his wife before they could eat of the tree of life.

In God's judgment upon Satan and his deception, God cursed the serpent and made a second promise. God promised that the seed of the woman would crush the head of the serpent and that the serpent would bruise his heel. This promise foretold God's deliverance of man from Satan's power through Christ's death and resurrection.

God then cursed the ground because of man's rebellion, man's sin. God told the man and his wife that because of their sin, their lives would become hard and full of painful labor all of the days of their lives. Then God took His most drastic step in His judgment on man's sin. He blocked the way to the tree of life. Because of his sin, man no longer had free access to eternal life. Man would die because of his sin, because of his rebellion against God.

The sin nature, the natural tendency to rebel against authority, had now taken up residence in the body of man. Sin now lived in man's flesh. However, it did not just live in man; it took control of man and enslaved man to sin. Paul's account of this sad situation of the unregenerate man is set forth for us in Romans 7:14, "I am of flesh, sold into bondage to sin." He continues in verse 17, "So now, no longer am I the one doing it, but sin which dwells in me."

Finally in verse 18 Paul says, "For the desire to do what is good is with me, but there is no ability to do it" (HCSB). Fortunately for the born-again believer, through the empowering of the indwelling of the Holy Spirit, there is the ability to do every good thing that the Lord commands us to do.

Man's access to the tree of life is blocked because of the sin of rebellion that man committed and because sin is now in man. By Christ's life, death, and resurrection, the blood that Christ shed paid the price for the sins that man has committed. The power of Satan, sins dominion over man, was also broken through Christ's death and resurrection. However, sin still remains in man's flesh, preventing man from receiving eternal life.

By believing in Christ Jesus as Lord, man is born again by the Holy Spirit making man's spirit alive and coming to dwell in it. God gives His Holy Spirit to the believer as a guarantee of the inheritance of the promises that God has made, if man remains in Christ, faithfully enduring unto the end, even unto death. The indwelling Holy Spirit empowers the believer to be holy, living a life in faithful obedience to Christ. This Spirit also pours out the love of God into the believer's heart enabling the believer to love God and to love one another as Christ has commanded them.

Many believe that a believer receives eternal life when they are born again. There are several verses that seem to indicate this. However, upon closer examination, we see that the meaning of these verses suggests otherwise.

One of these verses is John 3:36 which says, "He that believeth on the Son hath everlasting life: and he that believeth not the Son shall not see life; but the wrath of God abideth on him" (KJV). Another is John 6:47 which says, "Verily, verily, I say unto you, He that believeth on me hath everlasting life" (KJV).

The word "hath" in these verses is translated from the Greek word "echo" meaning "to hold," referring to the ability or condition of holding. In other words, it refers to something that you have the ability to receive if the required conditions are met. It is reminiscent of John 1:12 which says, "But as many as received Him, to them He gave the right to become children of God, even to those who believe in His name."

Believers now have the full promises of God restored to them. They now have the opportunity, through faithful obedience, to receive all of God's promises, including eternal life. The believer is back to a situation very similar to that of Adam in the garden of Eden. Adam had two sources of life that he could choose to live by. Adam could choose to live by the fruit of the tree of the knowledge of good and evil, or he could choose to live by the fruit of the tree of life.

One, the tree of the knowledge of good and evil, where God is disrespected and disobeyed, where man is enabled to live in whatever way seems right to him, the end of which is death. The other, the tree of life, where God is believed and trusted as one that is good and wants the best for man, the end of which is eternal life.

The born-again believer has now a similar situation. He has two natures, two different sources according to which he can choose to live. He can choose to live according to the flesh, or he can choose to live according to the Spirit.

He is no longer a slave to sin, under sin's control and domination. He can however choose to disrespect God and disobey God and live according to the lustful desires of the flesh, which leads to death. Or he can choose to believe God, trusting and honoring God as one that is good and desires and promises to provide only the best for man. The believer does this by living a life in humble obedience to the indwelling Holy Spirit, resulting in sanctification, the end of which is eternal life (Romans 6:22) .

Paul writes in 1 Corinthians 15:50, "Now I say this, brethren, that flesh and blood cannot inherit the kingdom of God; nor does the perishable inherit the imperishable." We will be changed. In a moment, in the twinkling of an eye, at the last trumpet, the dead will be raised incorruptible, and we will be changed.

When we are born again, we obtain an inheritance. Ephesians 1:11 says, "We have obtained an inheritance, having been predestined according to His purpose who works all things after the counsel of His will." He has given the ability through the empowering of the indwelling Holy Spirit to eventually, if we endure to the end, receive the inheritance that has been promised to the faithful, to the victor.

When we were born again, God qualified us by placing us into Christ to receive the inheritance among the saints. Colossians 1:12 says, "Giving thanks to the Father, who has qualified us to share in the inheritance of the saints in Light." Colossians 3:24 says, "From the Lord you will receive the reward of the inheritance."

Hebrews 12:17 says of Esau who sold his birthright, "For you know that even afterwards, when he desired to inherit the blessing, he was rejected, for he found no place for repentance, though he sought for it with tears." May none of us be like Esau who failed to understand the significance of his birthright and therefore did not value it as something extremely precious. Instead, he sold his birthright for a bowl of stew.

Eternal life is the birthright of every born-again believer. May we reflect on how precious this birthright of ours really is. May we value it above all else. Jesus tells us in John 17:3, "This is eternal life, that they may know You, the only true God, and Jesus Christ whom You have sent."

This is exactly what Paul was talking about in Philippians 3:8 where he says, "I count all things to be loss in view of the surpassing value of knowing Christ Jesus my Lord, for whom I have suffered the loss of all things, and count them but rubbish so that I may gain Christ." Again, in verse 10 Paul says, "That I may know Him and the power of His resurrection and the fellowship of His sufferings, being conformed to His death; in order that I may attain to the resurrection from the dead."

Paul writes in I Corinthians 13, "For now we see only a reflection as in a mirror; then we shall see face to face. Now I know in part; then I shall know fully, even as I am fully known." When Jesus returns, we shall see Him face to face. When He returns, and the veil of our flesh is removed and we shall know Him as fully as we are known.

1 Peter 3:9 says, "You were called for the very purpose that you might inherit a blessing." Is there any greater blessing than this, that we may know Him, that we might inherit eternal life? This is the purpose for which we have been called.

1 Peter 1:3-4 says, "Blessed be the God and Father of our Lord Jesus Christ, who according to His great mercy has caused us to be born again to a living hope through the resurrection of Jesus Christ from the dead, to obtain an

inheritance which is imperishable and undefiled and will not fade away, reserved in heaven for you."

Matthew 19:29 says, "And everyone who has left houses or brothers or sisters or father or mother or children or farms for My name's sake, will receive many times as much, and will inherit eternal life." Jesus said in Mark 10:29-30, "I assure you there is no one who has left house, brothers or sisters, mother or father, children, or fields because of Me and the gospel, who will not receive 100 times more, now at this time – houses, brothers and sisters, mothers and children, and fields, with persecutions – and eternal life in the age to come" (HCSB).

Matthew 25:34 says, "Then the King will say to those on His right, 'Come, you who are blessed of My Father, inherit the kingdom prepared for you from the foundation of the world.'" 1 John 2:25 says, "This is the promise which He Himself made to us: eternal life."

In Revelation 2:7, Jesus promises to give the victorious Christian in the church in Ephesus the right to eat of the tree of life. He says, "Anyone who has an ear should listen to what the Spirit says to the churches. I will give the victor the right to eat from the tree of life" (HCSB).

John tells us in Revelation 21:1-5, "Then I saw a new heaven and a new earth; for the first heaven and the first earth passed away, and there is no longer any sea. And I saw the holy city, new Jerusalem, coming down out of heaven from God, made ready as a bride adorned for her husband. And I heard a loud voice from the throne, saying, 'Behold, the tabernacle of God is among men, and He will dwell among them, and they shall be His people, and God Himself will be among them, and He will wipe away every tear from their eyes; and there will no longer be any death; there will no longer be any mourning, or crying, or pain;

the first things have passed away.' And He who sits on the throne said, 'Behold, I am making all things new.'

"The victor will inherit these things, and I will be his God and he will be My son" (Revelation 21:7, HCSB).

May we each endure to the end, loving nothing or no one more than our Lord Jesus Christ, that we might reign with Him and inherit all the blessings that God has promised to the faithful, to The Victorious Christian!

Chapter 18 Discussion Questions: Inheriting the Promises

1. What was God's first promise to man?
2. How was God's first promise to man communicated to him?
3. What happened before man ate of the tree of life?
4. How did Satan deceive the woman?
5. Why did the man sin?
6. What was God's second promise to man?
7. What was God's judgment on man for his sin of rebellion?
8. What causes man to sin today?
9. How do we know that Romans 7 is referring to the unregenerate man?
10. Why did God block man's access to the tree of life?
11. How do we know that the Greek word "echo" does not refer to something we already possess?
12. The promises of God are restored to believers. What must they do to inherit them?
13. What is the birthright of every born-again believer?
14. What did Jesus say in John 17:3 was eternal life?
15. What is the birthright of the born-again believer?
16. When will the victorious Christians receive eternal life?
17. What does God promise in Revelation chapter 21?